Patsy Brookshire

Threads

by

Patsy Brookshire

Threads

© 2006 by Patricia L. Brookshire

Another Touch-My-Heart production by
Ruby Rose Truckstop Enterprises
Brookport@peak.org

Manufactured in the United States.

Cover Design: Andrew E. Cier with Newport Lazerquick.
Front cover photo of Anna Gagne-Hawes,
courtesy of Greg Chaney.

ISBN: 10 1512398004
ISBN: 13 9781512398007
Library of Congress Control Number: 2006906074

1. Romance
2. Murder
3. Mystery
4. Quilting
5. Oregon beach

E-Published by Uncial Press,
An imprint of GCT, Inc.
Visit us at http://www.uncialpress.com

DEDICATION

To Bob Chaney

Thank you for reading Threads, supporting, encouraging,
and teaching me how to change a tire
in case I should ever need to.

ACKNOWLEDGEMENTS

One thinks when one writes a book that one made it all happen by oneself, but then a window in one's brain opens up...good heavens, it took a bunch of folks to complete this project! Therefore I say thank you to:

Sharon Bushard whose encouragement was constant, and whose spirit is my constant guide.

Readers and editors, in alphabetical order:

Gloria Miller Allen, Michelle Annette, Sharon Bushard, Bob Chaney, Fara Darland, Terry Goldade, Monica Goubaud, Susie Hatlevig, Avis Nelson, Perry Sams, Barbara Utterback, Chantall VanWey, and Dorothy Voreis. Of particular mention for her unerring attention to detail is Bonnie Brylinsky Chaney.

The incredibly patient women of our Focus writing group who listened, and critiqued this work: Margaret Arvanitis, Kelli Brugh, Mariah Matthews, Karleene Morrow and Sunshine Keck, I hope to give as much back to you.

My eleven aunts who, though none of them is Aunt Sophie, each contributed spirit and talent, giving life to her character, and who each, in her own way, encouraged me: Mary, Mabel, Lena, Lily, Bessie, Jessie, Virginia, Joy Brookshire; Wyona, Irene, Nellie Lackey. My six uncles, although none of them are Zack or Willie, did work these lives: Bill, Ernie, Edgar, Bob, Derl Brookshire; Morris Lackey.

My son Greg Chaney and my daughter Jennifer Chaney Morley Haggerty Connor, for your lifetime of patience with this and other writing projects.

My mother, Helen Louise Lackey Burton Brookshire, my father, Clarence Wilbur Brookshire and, sister Wanda Burton Bondi, from whose lives I took pieces for this story.

Curves women and co-workers who listened, and encouraged me with words and purchase! Rose Reed and Andrew E. Cier, of Newport LAZERQUICK who were patient and helpful.

To my Uncial Press editor, Judith B. Glad, I am everlastingly grateful for your touch of consistency and clarity. Thank you.

Last but never least, thank you husband John for morning coffee and the writer-sustaining gifts that you give me.

CONTENTS

Part 2

1. I'VE NEVER TOLD ANYONE

*S*he told me the story only once, over that Labor Day weekend, with such vividness and determination that I feel compelled to re-tell it, so that we can know the finality of it, and forgive the fragility.

Usually her tales were told as she worked about the house, or on her quilts. This one began that mid-Friday afternoon as we were picking blackberries. It was a beautiful September day, the time of year in Oregon when the seasons hang suspended--no longer summer, not yet fall.

Though she was old, her back was still straight and her face had a rosy, girlish joy as the berries piled up in the pail attached to her low-slung belt. A bee swung a bit too close to her face and she pulled back involuntarily, scratching her hand on the sharp briars.

"Cottonpickin' thunderbolts!" She shook her hand and sucked at the bit of blood that welled up. She laughed easily to herself, then looked over at me. Her rosy cheeks and soft black eyes--she was pretty, as I'd never seen her before. I'd never seen her as pretty, or homely, she was just Aunt Sophie, always there, and always the same.

"Annie," she said, a question in her tone, "did I ever tell you about David?"

I searched the family quickly, no David came to mind.

"No, of course I didn't," she went on, "I've never told anyone."

"Who is David?" I prodded as she seemed to sink into reflection. Was this a hint of the senility I was now on the lookout for?

"Aw, David," she said as if the name felt good on her tongue. She tasted it again. "David Andrew Smithers."

I could tell that the "Smithers" part didn't taste as well.

"Smithers," she said again, her lips wrinkling then smoothing with her smile. "Aw, well, he couldn't help that."

"What's wrong with 'Smithers'," I pressed, anxious lest she dismiss the whole thing before I found out who this David Andrew was that made her smile so.

"It's not artistic enough. David was an artist." Here she broke off. "How about we sit in the shade for a while?"

There were still lots of berries on the vines. Aunt Sophie never stopped until every container available, plus her apron, was full, so I quickly agreed, knowing that this tale was somehow different, important. We settled ourselves on a grassy spot and leaned against the trunk of a large fir.

"Now," I asked lightly, "who is David Andrew Smithers?"

"David was mine."

2. I KNOW YOU'RE BUSY, BUT...

It's unnerving to realize that I am not completely in charge of my future, that the past events and decisions made by another person can then wriggle their way into my life, affecting what I do today, and, what I do tomorrow. Such as the effect of these old, yellowed letters of Aunt Sophie's. You wouldn't think the words of a fourteen-year-old boy could spur me to spending my evenings at this typewriter, compelled to catch quickly the story of a family, most of whose members are long dead. I would much rather be out taking pictures or looking at the full moon with Roger, but as Aunt Sophie used to say, "First things first, Annie!" Agitating.

It's midwinter now and the rain of the last week has let up to just a soft dripping from the eave over my bedroom window to the flower bed below, pooling in the dirt under the cedar chips. The fresh smell through the open window is a pleasant accompaniment to the annoying hum of this old typewriter. My entrance into the story I have to tell began on quite another day, just prior to an unusually warm Labor Day weekend a few years ago.

I had dropped by Aunt Sophie's place for just a few minutes after work to see if there was anything she needed before I left for the holiday. The old gal threw me a curve. She asked me to spend the whole weekend with her. When I reluctantly agreed, I never intended to remain the full three days.

I had loosely arranged to spend Sunday and Monday nights in
the mountains with Len.

Len. Another memory, but at the time he was very current
and, I thought, was my future. By the stream by day and the cabin
fire by night we would have "A wonderful experience", "Get to
know each other better", and, I hoped, clear up some difficulties in
our relationship.

And then Aunt Sophie, with her clear-eyed logic, said, "Annie,
you're twenty-two and soon will be tied down with this Len
fellow." She could never just say, "Len". "...and won't have time
for your old auntie. You'll be busy with a house, and kids, and
what all, and before you know it I'll be gone." She knew I hated
any references to her age, or death. It was an effective way to get
to me.

"Of course, I know you're busy, and you young people do
have your own lives to live...."

I brushed that aside, even though I agreed with her.

"But I found a late patch of blackberries back in the woods
yesterday, and, you know, what with my hip and all, I didn't get
any jam or pies put up this year, and I just thought, wouldn't it be
nice if Annie and I could do those up together." She was pulling all
my strings now. "Remember when you were just little and weren't
much more than a bother, and how you loved to help me?"

So I told her I'd see if I couldn't work something out, some
time in, but I couldn't promise more than to see if I could get off
work early at the photo shop. That would give us Friday afternoon
and all Saturday but I already had plans for Sunday and Monday.

She seemed happy at that and I went home to my apartment
not thinking much more about it. But late that night, after having
suffered through an inane TV program while I waited, in vain, for
Len--sensitive, emotional, black-haired, black-eyed Len, whom I
planned to marry in the spring--to call, I went to bed. Instead of the
sleep I craved, I started thinking about my aunt.

Threads

Aunt Sophie was nearing eighty. Our age difference had never mattered. She'd always been my best friend, the one who taught me how to dress: "Be neat, Annie. Simple, but always put a little thought into your clothes, a little flair."

She analyzed my shape. "You're going to be tall. You'll be able to wear just about anything, but stay away from frills. They'll just make you look silly. With that blond hair of your mother's, and your dad's sweet mouth you don't need to look any... Well, you're something enough."

She undertook to study my character. "You're going to make mistakes," she told me one afternoon as she held me to her soft chest and patted me on the back. I'd come home heartsick because I'd told a secret a friend had trusted me not to tell, and the friend had found me out. I was sad, and embarrassed. "But use them to improve yourself."

"Here," she took her hankie--white lace, it was--from where she always carried it in the belt of her housedress, and wiped my eyes with the so-soft cloth. Her sturdy hands were old even then, lightly dusted with brown spots. Purple veins from her wrists traced down her fingers. Long, wide hands, worker hands. Laying her face against my wet cheek, she said, "Dear Annie," and kissed me quickly.

"Friendship is so fragile, but somebody will trust you again, and, next time you will do better. I have faith in you." She said this firmly, so that I believed her.

With Aunt Sophie shaping me like a tender young pear tree, pruning here and there, and propping up my fragile limbs, I grew strong enough to stand up on my own, and felt that I could weather any storms.

She was old-fashioned but she was the only one who took the time to care, to notice me.

I owed her a lot.

I loved her deeply.

5

3. ELM BRANCHES

Great Aunt Sophie was my father's mother's sister. She never married, so was sometimes referred to as, "Poor Aunt Sophie," at least by the more charitable members of the Elm family. This was a short list: two cousins of mine who left Oregon to move to faraway New York at a young age, to return to the bosom of the family in their late forties, long after Aunt Sophie's prime years. Someone else in the family, I remember Great Uncle Zack in particular, would snort, and say, "Poor Aunt Sophie my eye! I wish I could have got somebody to support me the way she did."

Aunt Sophie earned her keep. She lived with almost everyone in the family at one time or other and made a quilt for each of them. The quilts were personalized, depicting something close to the receiver's heart. They were beautiful.

Other than the New York cousins and myself, my Uncle Boyd was the only other relative who spoke up in his aunt's defense, and he did so from the distance of Washington, D.C. He provided her with the home she had lived in since she was in her fifties.

The Elm family had many branches--sorry, it's a family joke. Great Aunt Sophie, known to us simply as Aunt Sophie, had three brothers, Trevor, Zack, and Willie and four sisters, Lucy, Lydia, Mandy, and Herminie. Two of the brothers, Zack and Trevor, had never married.

Trevor never had a chance. In late 1917, at age seventeen, he went off enthusiastically to join the "War to End All Wars." By the spring of 1918 he was dead, shot, it was said, by a French housewife. The full story was never known and the family didn't seek details, it being enough to cope with the fact that Trevor had been dispatched by an ally. But it wasn't hard to figure out. Trevor had been a terror at home with a number of neighboring women and girls, so the family had reason not to look or question too closely.

Scandal was abhorred by the Elms. "Ignore the unpleasant or uncomfortable" was almost a family motto. The grief this caused can never be measured, certainly Aunt Sophie paid a high price to maintain it.

Trevor's death shocked the family but particularly left its mark on his younger brothers, especially Zack who took it bitterly. Ever afterwards his affection for anyone or anything was tempered with a grim reserve. He must have secretly admired Trevor's rough reputation but didn't have the guts to carry it off, just enough to be dangerous when thwarted.

Zack never married. He remained highly visible within the family, passionately unmarried, but he always had a girlfriend, a new one. Never seemed able to make up his mind whether he loved women, or hated them.

We sisters were wary of him. If one of us admitted she'd made a mistake about anything, big or small, he'd sneer, "Just like a woman." In private, he would borrow money that he seldom repaid. We stopped loaning him money after a while, which, of course, made him mad at us. He was our brother, so we loved him, but we didn't trust him.

The other brother, my Great Uncle Willie, married young but only had two children, the New York cousins, before he was killed in a logging accident in 1925. His wife sold their small farm, took the girls to the big city and made a small splash of brilliant spangles in what the family snidely described as "The Theater."

Two of Aunt Sophie's sisters, Lucy and Lydia, were twins.

Each married boys they knew from town and produced three children, whom they neglected and smothered in spurts, depending on whether they were drinking heavily or rediscovering religion. They did both frequently. The third sister, Herminie, married late, being nearly twenty-seven. For a while it had been feared she would be another poor spinster like Sophie. But she married a good man and had one child, the only real criminal the family ever produced. The boy was attracted to what he considered stagnant money in banks. He'd been unable, after stealing it, to resist setting fire to the building, using the President's desk as a base, and wills, mortgages and the like for tinder. He wasn't brought up much in family discussions.

The pride of the family though, for having kids, was my Grandmother Mandy, who married at fifteen and in the next twenty-five years gave birth to eighteen children, one of whom was my father. Only fourteen of them survived entry into the family, but these fourteen grew from healthy and lusty kids into healthy, lusty and often hell-raising, adults. Naturally enough these children of Mandy's, and the other married sisters and brother, produced even more children. Aunt Sophie was never without resources.

As Mandy's older sister, Sophie's career started naturally enough with the birth of Araminta, Mandy's first child. Mandy was barely sixteen and nervous about the whole affair. Her husband Zed, my grandfather, ran the local bar. He spent the event in town. His customers helped him celebrate the birth.

Aunt Sophie delivered the child and declared her to be, "Rather ugly but she has nice hands and feet." Despite Mandy's protests she stayed to help with the canning and never returned home.

By late 1918 Mandy had four children. Aunt Sophie had helped birth them all, including number four, my father, Wilber.

For some reason no one knew but everyone gave thanks for, Mandy didn't have any children for the next few years. Some cynics said that with the war over Zed didn't need to keep producing dependents. Whatever the reason, it gave everyone a much needed rest, at least temporarily.

Aunt Sophie stayed until Wilber was walking and then, with
no new births on the horizon, she went to Cannon Beach, where
Willie and Zack were working on the roads. She kept house for
them for some months and "worked out" for a couple of years.
That was the story the family knew, and the one I'd grown up with.
I never suspected, because I was, naturally more interested in
myself than in her life, that there was more to those years than I
knew. Incredibly more.

In that time she knew love.

4. WALKING CAREFULLY

You know that Mandy had Zed, and the twins had Jack and Edward, and even Hermie eventually got her Zorba." Sophie wasn't asking me. It was a statement of fact.

I nodded.

"Well, David was mine."

She took a deep breath, settling herself more firmly onto the ground. "He was mine, but he belonged to someone else."

This is Sophie's story, hers and David's.

* * * *

The winter your father was learning to walk, I got a letter from Zack. He and Willie were batching it in a small cabin at Cannon Beach. Zack wanted me to come down and keep house for them. The ocean was beautiful in winter, he said, and they had a grand view from their window. It would be a big help if I could just add a feminine touch to the place. He meant do all their womanly work for them, of course.

It sounded romantic to me, and Mandy had been kinda testy lately. The winter supplies were in and she could handle the kids and Zed by herself, now that she was all of twenty, so I went.

When I got there it was the middle of November, but warm. The cabin was bigger than I expected, with two small bedrooms. Willie and Zack shared one and I had the other one all to myself. After all the years of sharing a bed with either a sister or one of Mandy's kids, it felt good to have a whole bedroom all to myself, let alone my own bed. It was just a simple cot, with a straw mattress. I wanted to make a quilt for it so Willie made me a frame to work on. While the boys were at work, after I had my chores done, I'd get out my scrap bag, which goes everywhere I do, and cut pieces.

The boys were glad to have me. They were only seventeen and sixteen that first winter. Willie especially missed the motherly nagging, though you'd never have known it to hear them talk. They loved being on their own and making their own pay. They blew half of their wages every Saturday night at the dance hall saloon in Seaside.

Before I came they blew almost all of it. After a couple of bad weekends I made them give me half of it before they went to town. They didn't like it but it was the only way I could make sure we had food on the table and the rent got paid. After rent, food, savings for all three of us, and a wage to me, the rest was theirs. I marked three envelopes, one for Willie, one for Zack, and one for myself and put in three dollars a week in each of the envelopes. Zack never really appreciated it, especially the money I kept as wages for myself, two dollars a week.

Naturally, he made the most work for me. Zack still thinks women were born to serve him, which is why he never got a women to stay with him for long. Our natures were never very sympathetic to each other. I fancied myself a suffragette and resented his attitude towards me.

I have to admit this too, I liked my position as older sister. I made the most of the opportunity to boss Zack around without Mom there to interfere. He fought me, but because he had asked me to come, he had little ground to stand on. Not if he wanted dinner.

Willie was different. He was grateful for everything I did for him. Zack was a terrible cook and housekeeper so Willie was delighted with the clean cabin and my apple pies, thick bean soups and the chowders I learned to make.

The kitchen was mine. Not Mandy's or my mother's. Mine. I filled the windowsills with shells from the things we caught and that we found. There was a mist of sand on the sills from the wind through the cracks around the window frames. The stove worked best for me; the boys could never get it right. And then I would show them how to build the right kind of fire. It irritated them, which was of course why I did it. That was my most favorite kitchen, even more than David's. The boys were more than glad to have me take over.

They taught me how and where to dig for the razor clams on the beach. And how to get the blue-shelled mussels that we steamed and dipped in melted butter. Mmm, so good.

We got the mussels from the rocks and the tide pools at Haystack when the water was just covering them. Most of the time I could twist them off the rocks; sometimes I had to use a knife to cut them loose. Whenever the tide was right or I was tired of beans and smoked pork, I'd take my shovel and knife down to the beach and get mussels and all kinds of clams. The smell of salt in the air, the sun shining on my back, or the fog swirling around... I still miss it.

We went fishing in the surf when it wasn't too rough. We had fish fried, baked, and in soup, until we were sick of it and glad to get back to bread and beans. Once in a while we took a little boat and went crabbing. I don't know who the boat belonged to. It sat up above the beach and we'd just put it back when we were done. Zack made a crab pot out of some wire and net he got from a fisherman friend. It was a round thing that you throw in the water weighted with some fishing lead. We'd tie some stinky fish to the net and throw it in the water from the boat, come back about an hour or so later and pull it up. One of my jobs was to dip the bucket we brought along into the ocean, leaning over the edge of the boat and scooping it about half full of water.

Truth to tell, I loved going out over the waves onto the ocean.
It was just scary enough to be fun, but I trusted the boys to be able
to get us out and back. Didn't do it often 'cause the ocean was
pretty rough most of the time.

Getting crabs was fun, like a surprise party every time we
pulled that thing up. They'd be scooting around in there trying to
get out and Zack would just grab 'em and throw 'em in the bucket. I
was scared they'd grab me. They'd scritch and scratch around in
there until we got 'em home and put 'em out of their misery by
throwing them in a pot of boiling water. Cooked in the salt water
I'd got from the ocean, with a bit of nutmeg, they weren't bad but I
never was crazy about them like the boys were. And David.

Willie shot a deer just before Thanksgiving, soon after I came.
What we didn't eat fresh I made into venison mincemeat, with
raisins and pieces of apple with a good amount of vinegar to tart it
up. It made great pies. I canned a bunch of it up. Some Sundays I'd
make a couple mincemeat pies. Willie'd hang around to smell them
cooking. But more, he did love it when I'd give him a big slice. I'd
watch him eat it, smacking his lips. I maybe enjoyed it more than
he did.

Both the boys were rough. That was the way with all the men
in our family, I didn't think much about it. Their manners were
terrible. They belched at the table and never excused themselves.
Their hands were callused and unclean looking from the rough
road work they did. I made them wash for meals. They had to be
reminded to comb their hair, except on Saturday nights, and the
only clothes they had were work clothes, the red plaid shirts and
dark work pants.

On Saturday night, Zack, in particular, had a regular ritual of
cleaning up. He washed his hands and face real good, changed his
work socks for his nicer, dancing socks. Most of all, he polished
his shoes, his special dancing shoes, something the other guys-
certainly not Willie--didn't have. He'd get out his black polish and
his special rag, and after cleaning off the stuff left on his shoes
from the week before, he whip those dancing shoes into shape-you
know, polish and spit, polish and spit. When he got done he'd

put those shoes on and walk different. Careful not to get in any mud. He carried a piece of cloth in his pocket to spiff them up just before he and Willie went into the hall.

There was a dance hall over to Seaside where everybody went. The boys had an old buggy that one of the guys from the road crew got from somebody. They'd all go over in that. I didn't much like the road, as it was close to the cliffs in a couple places, rough cut and narrow. They guys all had the same idea of a great time, going to the dance hall with plenty of liquor and dancing with the wild girls they met there.

Sometime early in the morning one of the guys from Seaside would dance with one of the girls that belonged to a guy from the road crew and she would laugh too much at his jokes. The fight would be on. It was the same every Saturday night. Willing girls, too much whisky, wild dancing, then the fight. The ride home was a sobering experience with the trees leaning in close and who knows what out there in the dark. At least the horses only drank water so everybody always made it home in one piece.

I know all this because I went with them. I liked the dancing, and yes, the drinking. The men all had strong arms and spared no expense at showing a fun-loving gal a good time. They were young and so was I. My hair was down to the middle of my back, and dark. Ebony-black David called it. I was taller then, five feet seven. A couple of inches, maybe, have disappeared. I was full-hipped, not just broad like now, and high breasted, and my waist was small so it narrowed-in nicely. The men liked to grab me around the middle and twirl me around. Even David liked to run his hands down my sides. "Measure the hourglass," he'd say.

I was never especially pretty, but I was what they called then, handsome. But David said that when I laughed, I was beautiful.

David lived in the house above us. It wasn't a cabin. It was a real house that David and his wife had designed and built themselves. They got wood from all sorts of places, some that washed up on the beach, some lumber they bought from Seaside, and then David had cut down trees up in the woods. The house was much longer than it was wide. It faced the ocean and was a two-storied affair with what they called a cupola on top, right in the middle.

The cupola looked like a fancy chicken coop to me. It was glass all around, except for the wooden frame. You could open up the window front and back to let the air blow through. David loved to sit up there in the summer and paint. Painting was the way he made his living, and it was his passion. When he tired of painting he would turn to his telescope and watch the seals over by Ecola Bay.

The second floor was their bedroom. There was also a smaller bedroom, which was meant to be a child's room, but, in their twelve years of marriage, no children had come. They used it mostly for storing David's paintings.

The downstairs was one big, long room. The kitchen was at one end and a big stone fireplace was at the other end. The fireplace had a double chimney that opened into their bedroom, too.

There was a big window near the front door, with a long bench in front of it. The bench was painted yellow, and had a large Christmas cactus sitting on one end. The cactus brightened that corner with red blossoms at odd times throughout the year. I remember violets and geraniums in that window, too. All kind of plants new to me.

My folks never had much use for plants in the house, things needed to be useful. This was my first experience that I could like things different from my family. The colorful plants were useful in cheering dark winter days, as was the large window that provided light for them. The plants did well.

Most surprising to me was the bookcase. We didn't have much cause or time for reading at home, so almost a whole wall for books was odd to me. Against the back wall, it reached from floor to ceiling. The supports were hand-notched. In bare places were a few knickknacks, but mostly shells. Lots of shells.

In the few feet of space not taken up by the bookcase was a

small, paned window looking back over the property into trees. In winter, with some of the trees and bushes bare, you could see if someone passed by on the road above. Under the window was the sewing machine, beside which was a large humpbacked trunk, used for storing material and Amy's sewing stuff.

Over by the front door was where everybody hung their coats and hats, and all sorts of other things: buckets, clamming shovels, a lantern. I've forgotten what all. David kept saying he was going to build a porch to hide it all proper-like, but he never did.

I didn't meet David until spring came, but I saw him every day. A path led from his house to the beach and it passed within a few feet of our cabin. I didn't notice him for the first two or three days. I was too busy cleaning and cooking, but soon after I had the household setting into a routine, I noticed him.

I was standing at the window watching the ocean. It was early, about 6:00 a.m. The morning light was just starting to show. It was stormy as I remember, not like it gets in mid-winter, but I'd lived inland all of my life and never seen any kind of sea storm so I was fascinated. Seagulls were out there flying into the wind, catching updrafts and in general just having a good time. When I saw something move out of the corner of my eye, I turned and looked.

A man was walking slowly right by our cabin, carefully so as not to slip on the slick grass. Once in a while he would look down to check his footing, but mostly he walked with his head high. He was looking all around, feeling the wind and smelling the air, but when he walked past my window he looked away. So he wouldn't be staring in our place, you know.

He was very polite, David was.

5. WHO IS THAT FELLOW?

I couldn't see his face because he was going away from me, but I looked him over careful. I was already twenty-two years old, remember, and I'll admit it, every man was a possibility. He wasn't tall--five feet eight and a half inches--and even dressed like he was I could tell he didn't have much meat on him.

He had on a heavy oilskin coat like fishermen wear, and high rubber boots. The hood of his coat was thrown back but an old, yellow sou'wester protected his neck and ears from the wind. His pants were black, and lumpy, like he had another pair under them. His hands were stuffed in his pockets most of the time, 'cept when he took them out to steady himself. He looked like a fisherman but he didn't have a pole, so I wondered what he was doing.

I watched him go down the path, slow and careful, until he disappeared 'round the bend. I went to the front window and kept watching. Pretty soon I saw him walk out on the beach, right toward the waves. I thought for a minute that maybe he was crazy, you know, going to walk right out there and drown himself or something, but then I thought, he's too dressed up for that, unless he wants to die warm. But he just walked at the water's edge for a long way down the beach 'til I got bored watching. I got the broom and started sweeping sand from the floor to out the door.

The sand. Always sand on the floor. Nearly drove me mad crunching underfoot and clinging to my shoes and hiding between my toes so that I always had to wash my feet before climbing into bed at night.

About an hour later I saw him coming back up the path. I stood at the window and watched him come. I guess I was kinda bold, but how else was I going to see his face if I didn't look at him? He was holding some shells, sand dollars I think, in one hand, and his poor hands looked cold and raw, and red. I didn't think he saw me, so I continued to stare at him.

I put my hand up to smooth my hair and I guess the motion caught his eye 'cause suddenly he looked up, straight at me. And he grinned.

He was no more than four feet away from me and that big grin just about turned my heart over. I didn't mind staring at him, but I didn't expect him to be bold right back.

His eyes were blue--bright blue topped by wild, bushy red eyebrows--and his teeth were very white. He had a red mustache that curled on the ends, but otherwise he was clean shaven. His face was raw from the wind, especially his cheekbones. His face all over was almost too sweet, but the sharp cheekbones and mustache gave him a dashing appearance. I still don't know whether it was the smile or his eyes that did me in.

I was so startled when he grinned at me that I was almost scared, but I couldn't help myself, I smiled right back. He nodded, then was gone past the cabin, up the path back to his strange house.

From then on I watched him nearly every day. He was as regular as the clock. Down the path at six, an hour on the beach, then back past the cabin about seven. Always, unless I was out clamming, or something, I stood there and watched him go by. And always he looked in at me and grinned.

He sometimes walked past near dusk but I usually ignored him then because the boys were there.

I was like a fascinated thing. I could no more keep away from that window than I could stop breathing.

I lived that winter on David's smiles. I thought of him during the day as I worked and I dreamed of him at night when I slept. I would be embarrassed to tell you about those dreams. When I got up at four in the morning, the thought that I would soon see him warmed me as I made the fire in the cook stove.

The boys didn't suspect a thing. On Saturday nights I went to the dances with them and had a good enough time, but I was always hoping he'd be there. He never was, of course. He was at home with his wife. I didn't know he had a wife. I'd blocked the possibility right out of my mind. David had no wife in my dreams, except maybe me. I didn't know until one day, in late winter, when David walked past one evening when I was staring out the window watching some gulls argue over something on the beach. It would have been unnatural to have ignored the fact that a man was walking right by the window, so I casually asked the boys, "Do you guys know who that fellow is?"

Zack looked up and snorted. "Sure, that's crazy Smithers."

"Crazy Smithers?" My heart dropped. But I tried to sound casual, like it was just an ordinary conversation and I didn't care much.

"Yeah," said Willie. "Some of the guys call him that 'cause he's a painter. But I don't think he's crazy."

"A painter?"

"Yeah, of pictures." He made a square with his hands like a frame.

My relief was confused. I wasn't sure a painter was a "real man."

19

You understand, don't you Annie?

"Well," said Zack, "if he's not crazy he's
probably...unnatural...which is just about the same thing."

I was feeling rather queasy.

"Naw, Zack," Willie said, "he's nothing… He's just different.
He uses his hands to make a living just like we do, 'cept he paints
with his. I saw him down to the beach a couple a times last
summer, painting. He was painting birds and people poking around
Haystack Rock and it looked real, real, you know, almost like a
photograph."

"Yeah?" Zack gave Willie a funny look. "That proves it, only
weird people mess around drawing pictures when they should be
working."

"No, you're wrong, Zack. I know it."

"Yeah? How?"

"He had his wife with him," Willie answered flatly.

My heart felt like a rock. I didn't know whether to be crushed,
or relieved.

"Yeah?" Women always interested Zack. "Is she a painter,
too? What's she look like?"

"I don't think so. She was just lying on a blanket in the sun.
She's kinda frail looking. Short, blonde hair and big brown eyes.
Little woman. There was something about her didn't seem too
strong. She was sorta pale, like she didn't get out much. But she
was real nice. Friendly. Sweet-like."

"Humph." You could tell Zack was thinking it over. "Still, I
wouldn't let the guys see you hanging around Smithers. They
might get wrong thoughts."

Willie let the subject drop but his mouth had the set look it got when he'd made up his mind he was going to do what he dang well pleased. But what Zack said must of stayed with him because next summer he avoided going down to the beach when he knew David was there.

6. THE BEACH IN WINTER

I wasn't idle that winter, though I certainly didn't keep a spotless house. That winter was not a problem of too little to do, but too much. Other than clammin' and fishing there was plenty of housework. Our water came from a rain barrel by the cabin, plus what the boys got from a well in town. We had a crude washing setup at the side of the cabin, with a couple tin tubs I washed and rinsed in. They'd put a rough roof over my wash area and strung up a couple clotheslines to a tree. I also had a couple lines in the house that I hung clothes on when it rained.

After the work was done, the cabin cleaned and bread set to rise, I'd get to work on my quilts. One for Zack, one for Willie, and finally, one for myself. Zack and Willie's were traditional: a design of plain squares for Zack, 'cause he didn't like anything too fancy, and a star quilt for Willie. His was many colored, with even some flower pieces from old dresses. I wouldn't dare use flowers on Zack's. He'd a burned it up.

Mine was different, big enough for a double bed, 'cause I still had hopes. But sort of modernistic, I guess you would call it now. I wanted to capture the ocean, but I couldn't get it right. I was trying to copy the seashore with a sandy gray, the sun with a bright yellow circle, and the different blues of the sky and the sea with broad bands of varied and pale violets, but it was defeating me.

The sky and the water looked different, depending on the weather. I particularly wanted to capture the sea as I'd seen it the first days after I arrived. The contrast in the weather--one day was brilliantly appealing, sunny and warm, and the next was foggy cold and windy--stunned me into a love for the sea that I've never lost, though I came to dread the many endless days of thick fog through the next long, lonely winter.

The boys had picked me up in the late afternoon from the train in Seaside, so that by the time we arrived at the cabin I'd seen only little glimpses of the ocean. The sun was low in the sky when I got my first full view of the shore.

We were carting my belongings down the path to the cabin. I stopped and looked at the ocean. In front of me was all blue and green water, moving and foamy, stretching 'til it met the faraway sky, which was a different blue, with clouds reflecting up the colors of water and sky.

In the center, just off shore, were three big rocks. The one in the middle was the biggest. The boys had told me about what they could see from the cabin windows. To Willie I said, "Haystack Rock? Is that it?"

"Of course," he said. "There's nothing around here like it." I threw my stuff on the floor, didn't even take a look around. Right then and there I challenged Willie and Zack to a race to the waves. They won. They were stronger and running through dry sand is hard.

Once I got on the wet, firm sand, I sprinted barefoot for the shallow water and ran splashing past the boys. The water rolled in to greet me, all foamy. I turned and ran down through the surf towards Haystack. It looked so close, but the distance was deceptive. Before long I was out of breath and little closer.

The boys caught up with me and we strolled through the shallow water, with me splashing it into a fine spray with my toes. It was cold, not like river water at home in the summer. When the sun started to set on the horizon, my brothers turned me around to walk up to a drier spot to sit on the sand and watch the sunset.

"Just look, Sophie!" Willie said, happy to have someone from home to show this off to, "Ain't it beautiful?"

The sun was a round, red blaze sinking into dazzling blue water, casting up a pink and pale blue sky before, above, and all around us.

"Ummm, Ummmm." was all I could say. So quickly, before I could absorb the glory, it was over. The sun flattened out like a stepped-on rubber ball, then slipped into the ocean.

"Couldn't you almost hear it sizzle?" whispered Zack as we stood silently in the twilight. He surprised me. Zack was not known for his sensitive nature. I couldn't resist the urge to tease him a bit.

"Why, Zack, I think you've got a poet's soul. Willie, did you hear what he said?"

"Ah-h-h, Soph," Willie kidded, using his childhood name for me, "leave the poor guy alone. A night like this would turn anyone's head, even a tough heart like Zack." Zack was glaring at both of us, saying nothing.

Poor Zack, he so seldom opened up like that, and we crushed him. As the now-oldest boy, no one ever let him forget that he had to see things clearly, with no romantic haze. We could be as silly as we wanted, but he must maintain a toughness, be a "real man". I hadn't learned yet that a real man could be both tough and tender.

We strolled home, getting to the cabin just as dark set in.

I went to bed early, bone tired from the ride and the play on the beach. Hours later I woke up. There were no windows in my room and it was dark and stuffy. I laid for a few minutes with the blankets thrown back, shaking the warm nightclothes away from my body, trying to whip up a cool breeze. The longer I laid there the heavier the air seemed. I could hear the boys in the next room, one of them snoring loudly, fairly shaking the front room window, the other breathing heavy in the close room. At first it was funny listening to them competing with the noisy ocean but I couldn't go back to sleep. They jangled my nerves until I finally got up and found my old robe in the dark. I felt my way through the curtain into the lighter front room.

Moonlight was forcing its way through the dirty window. The air was fresher in the larger room, but not much. Outside had to be better, and away from the snoring.

The night was warm and unusually dry. Willie had said it hadn't rained for days. The grass was sandy and dry under my bare feet. Away from the protection of the cabin, a fresh wind brushed my face and blew my hair against my neck.

Trees and beach alike were patterned in moon shadows bouncing off some dark clouds above. The moon was full and white. It lit the way easily. I walked to the lip of the little hill overlooking the beach, sat down carefully and gave myself up to the warm beauty of the night.

I was admiring the silhouette of Haystack and watching the waves breaking on the low tide when I noticed something I'd not seen in the daytime, white fire on the waves. As they broke and ran down the beach the foam shimmered. I held my breath as diamonds of fire sparkled on each wave.

On my far right I could see a faint twinkle of light from the ocean. At first I thought it was coming from a ship, then I realized it was from a rock out in the water. A lighthouse sitting on a rock in the sea, its light blinking in a steady rhythm.

I sat for a while soaking up the romantic atmosphere, feeling lonelier by the minute. It was a night made for love. A full moon, tide out, fresh warm air, running waves of fire shimmering on the dark sea, with only the single man-made light sparkling in the dark. I longed for a strong arm to pull me close, a bristly cheek to brush against my neck, tender hands and lips to share this moonlit night with. But try as I did, I couldn't conjure up a vision of anyone special I wanted with me.

Opening my eyes I took in the scene around me once more, sighed, and let my practical nature take over. It was long after midnight, I should be in bed. I'd left the cabin door open, and the fresh air had calmed the boys' dreams so that the cabin was peacefully quiet and cool. Sleep came easily.

Waking early the next morning I dressed quickly, went to the front room window and saw water, a wide, white beach of waves running far down both ways from the window. And rocks, huge rocks. Haystack was the biggest of all. In the distance to the right was the one with the lighthouse on it. They were scattered all up and down the coast just a little ways out from the surf, like dark guardians of the ocean. We had a grand view from that cabin.

I rushed through breakfast with the boys, packed their lunch buckets, and waved them off to work. As soon as they were gone I threw a light jacket and a scarf on and went out to a wonderful, sunny morning.

The tide was partially out. As soon as I got down the bank, I took off my shoes and left them there with my socks stuffed in. Who was going to steal them? Following the same route as the day before, I was determined to get to the big rock. It didn't seem as far away as before, probably because I was rested. The early morning beach was strewn with what I soon learned were sand dollars, round, white shells about three inches across, with an interesting design of five narrow ovals, finger-like markings spread from a base like sunrays. I put them in my pockets, along with lots of small, orange fan-shaped shells, and some other kinds, --'til my jacket pockets were full. I couldn't swing my arms for fear I'd crack the shells.

The ocean looked like a big turquoise cake with creamy white frosting spilling over the edge. The sky was flat with no color, clear, bright, no clouds whatsoever. From a distance, Haystack Rock shimmered green in the sun. Closer up I saw it was covered in a thick, dark green moss and a tough grass that grew out of cracks in the side of the rock. The base of the rock intrigued me most. I'd never seen a tide pool, or so many seagulls, or the little sandpipers.

They were so cute. I miss 'em. They hopped and pecked at the blue mussels and ivory barnacles that covered the rocks of the tide

26

pools.

The gulls squawked at me, and each other, and at the sandpipers, making a big show of protecting their rocks. They flapped away when I got too close. They'd settle down again on the rocks just a little farther away, screaming at me. I laughed, but the sandpipers took them seriously, skittering away across the sand, and then coming back when the gulls moved away. The little birds moved in a group but the gulls were more solitary, each bird for himself.

Some rocks close up beside Haystack, smaller but still big, reminded me of giant thumbs pointing towards the sky, a "thumbs up" position that further cheered me to the delights of the morning. I spent a couple of hours just looking at the tide pools full of little bitty crabs and swimmy things that dashed away when I tried to touch them. And anemones, squishy, purple, soft things that squeezed shut when I put my fingers on their sticky edges. The farm never had anything like this.

I was like a kid, wondering how everything worked and why the barnacles were so rough and hard while other things acted like animals when I touched them. I didn't know the names of things at first, of course, but the guys all told me the details over the time I was there. Men love to tell you everything they know.

But the sun was blinding white and despite the light breeze, the sleep I'd missed the night before caught up with me. I needed to go home before I fell asleep on the beach. The walk back was slow because I kept stooping to pick up gray and black feathers and more shells, and to look at the glass-like globs that were all over the beach. They juggled when I poked them with a black feather; I was afraid to touch anything that looked like it might be alive. Later the boys laughed at me being afraid of dead jellyfish.

By the time we went to bed that night the wind was really blowing through the trees, but it was hot and sleepless inside again. After getting the boys off to work in the morning I went back to bed and didn't get down to the beach until late. The tide was high, way in, and the wind was tearing down the beach. Even with one of Zack's heavy jackets on, the long walk towards Elk Creek up the other way, away from Haystack towards where the lighthouse light had shone, was cold, windy, and miserable. Shells were scarce and the wind threw sand in my face--it stung--so I had to keep my head down. I finally got to the creek, running fresh into the ocean, and happily turned to go home.

The wind pushed me back to the warm cabin. I added wood to the stove, and from my snug harbor watched the gulls flying into the wind and ocean tumbling onto the sand. I got out my quilt bag and played with cloth, fingering the pieces I had and comparing them with what I saw out the window.

To transfer all the moods and shades of the sea to simple cloth seemed about impossible. How to show the feeling of differences in the fogs? Dark, gray sky and water through a light fog was different from when the fog rolled in so thick that everything was gone, nothing but gray, coldness everywhere. I hated the thick fog, it closed me in. I felt trapped, shut off from the world. But the light fog, it's beautiful swirling in and around the trees, a thick layer of gray lace tangling lightly with the branches. Lovely too, because it would soon be gone, bringing, at least light, and sometimes, the precious sun.

There was hope in the light, despair in the thickness. I knew I'd have to make the back of my quilt a solid gray to represent the fog. "The Beach in Winter" I called it.

But the front piece was giving me fits. Until near spring when I remembered what Willie had said about David painting Haystack Rock.

That was it!

I'd put Haystack in the middle on a background of bright blue. The rock would be reddish brown, like it is sometimes when the evening sunset turns the sky red. Surrounding the big center square would be yellow suns, embroidered all the way 'round. The border would be a pale blue, quilted to look like waves.

I started with the Rock, as it was the central, most important piece, drawing its shape on a pad I had left from school and kept in my quilt bag. The Rock was in clear view from the front window, except when hidden by fog. I spent hours trying to copy it.

I couldn't get it. The harder I tried the worse it looked. I'd make it too big for anything else to be around it. I couldn't get how it looked with the whole of the sea and sky surrounding it. I spent many hours by the window sketching it in different weathers. Finally I put it away and went back to work on the boys' quilts.

7. WHAT ARE YOU DOING HERE...?

*A*long about the end of March the weather started clearing. It was still rainy and foggy most of the time, but the long winter was finally coming to an end.

After I learned that David was married, I wasn't at the window so often. For the first three days or so I hid in my bedroom when I saw him leave the beach below, and only came out when I was sure he'd had time to pass. But finally I could stand it no longer, I missed his smile too much.

If my romantic dreams couldn't come true I could at least be friendly. The poor man, I thought, stuck in the house with a sick wife, probably a whiney invalid. Perhaps our daily exchange was as important to his life as it was to mine--in a different way of course. By that time, David had assumed such saintly proportions that I couldn't conceive of him being unfaithful to his wife, however much a trial she was to him.

On the fourth day, I had gone into my bedroom as usual, but after a few minutes I spread the curtain cautiously and looked across the room out the window. David had just come in view and he was looking directly at the cabin. His face had a searching, troubled look and his shoulders were slumped.

I couldn't bear to see him like that. I came out and walked over to the window.

As soon as I appeared his whole appearance changed. His shoulders went back, his step was lighter and his face lit up in a big smile.

I was exhilarated and terrified. His hold on me was total, and I knew it. And we'd never even spoken a word. As he passed he stopped and said, "I missed you." Then he went on. I couldn't hear the words but I knew what he had said.

The rest of the day was a haze. I tried to sew, and couldn't. His words kept repeating in my brain, "I missed you. I missed you. I missed you." I had imaginary conversations with him where I went out the door and took his hands in mine and looking deep into his eyes said, I missed you, too.

Come away with me, he pleaded.

But your wife?

What wife? I have no wife.

But, the woman on the beach?

Oh, that was my sister who was ill and here for the sea air. She is gone now, so come and live with me in my beautiful house.

Gladly, I answered.

Thus I easily dismissed the wife. She didn't exist for David and me. Still I had sense enough to try to cool my behavior. I seldom stood at the window anymore. When he came by, I would be busy sweeping or kneading bread, or at the stove. He would get a nod or a slight wave but I kept my face busy, paying attention to the work I was doing. He must not know how completely he had me, how I lived each day to see him, a man I didn't even know.

'Round about the end of March, first of April, I started working outside on the garden. I would wait till David was home again and then go out. I cleared a large area of ground, pulling out ferns and salal, and roots. You wouldn't believe the roots. That ground had never been dug. Lucky it was so sandy. Still it was a hard job. It took a couple more days than I thought it would to get it done, and the main reason I got it done even then was because Willie and Zack each put in some time before dinner. They pounded those roots and chopped 'em till the whole patch was a fine mash. The sweat was just 'a flying! They turned it all over for me. By the end of April I had the garden put to peas and green beans and chunks of sprouted potato. I spaded up the dirt by the front door and around the cabin for flowers. It was inevitable that working near the path so often I would meet David.

I'd wondered at him never knocking on my door and introducing himself, as a neighbor might, or why he didn't just chance by when I was working on the garden. I, well... I don't think he was any more anxious to meet the real me than I was him. Dreams were a lot easier to deal with than reality, and too, David thought I was the wife of one of the boys.

On the first day of May I got up early. Spring was in the air and the morning was warm. I had a couple of rose bushes I'd bought the week before at the general store in town, red climbers, and I knew when I got up that this was the day to plant them.

David went by, at six as usual. I had my morning coffee and then, thinking I had plenty of time, went to the woodshed for the roses and spade. When I came back around to the front, David was coming up the path.

There was nothing to do but to act like it was a normal thing to see him there. To bolt into the house would have looked foolish. Standing there with the spade in one hand and a rosebush in the other, I said, "Morning!"

He stopped, startled. He'd been looking at the tiny yellow flowers by the path and hadn't seen me.

At my greeting he looked up, then came straight towards me, that big grin spreading on his face.

"Why, good morning to you." His voice was big for a small

man, and didn't sound in the least "unmanly". His hand was outstretched. I leaned my shovel against the cabin and put my hand into his, as natural as anything.

Young folks do it now but it wasn't something girls did then. I'd expected artistic hands with long narrow fingers but the hand in mine was compact, a worker's hand without calluses. It was a pleasant experience, but I was fearful for a second that he would say, "Come away with me." He didn't. He proceeded to talk like we were having a normal conversation.

I was shy being face-to-face with him so suddenly. He was almost a stranger. But he didn't act like one. He let go of my hand, and just as natural as if he were continuing a conversation we'd started a while ago, asked, "Planting the roses?"

I came out of my stupor enough to answer, "Why, yes," while my thoughts ran around searching for something smart to say. Nothing came.

"Right here by the door, I hope. That's the best place."

I nodded dumbly.

"Well, let's get at it." He lifted that shovel right out of my hand and started digging in the loosened dirt, covering my shyness with talk.

"My mother had roses, a whole arbor of them to the side of the house. I used to play out there under the roses, when I was just a little boy. It was cool there. I love roses, don't you?" Before I could answer he laughed, "Dumb question. Of course you do."

My mind was moving again, but I guess I was not in complete control, for I blurted out, "What are you doing here?" It sounded more like an accusation than a question. I immediately wished I'd kept my mouth shut but I've always been that way, "Mouth ahead of brain," my daddy used to say.

David stopped his digging, and looked directly at me. I tried to avoid his eyes.

"No, look at me."

I did, but it was uncomfortable even through the pleasure of looking so straight on at him.

"We--" he stopped. "What's your name?"

I stumbled it out.

"Sophie," he repeated, making it sound special. "I'm David."

I stood still, looking into his eyes, a fascinated thing like the hens would get when the boys petted them on their throats.

"Well, Sophie, I'm here to help you plant the roses. I came back up to get my paints. It's a natural day for painting, as it is for planting roses. But, I knew perfectly well that you would be here, maybe not today, but sometime. We couldn't go on forever seeing each other and never meeting, now could we?"

"Well... I never really thought about it." I mumbled the lie. This mumbling around was awful. He was going to think I was a complete idiot. Shrugging my shoulders in what I hoped was a casual manner I spoke up more firmly. "No, I guess not. After all," I said lightly, "we're neighbors."

"No Sophie, we're more than neighbors. I know it, don't you?"

I struggled against answering but his eyes demanded an answer. An honest answer, and for the life of me I couldn't lie to him. "Yes," then, angry at his forcefulness, I found my tongue. "If we're not just neighbors, what do you think we are?" I didn't want him examining what I thought we were.

"Friends," he answered. The dark blue eyes relaxed their grip on me and became sunny again.

"Friends, Sophie, and Lord knows that's as rare as, well, as rare as having an ebony-haired beauty greet me every day with a beautiful smile."

"Ebony-haired beauty?" Me?

I'd never had a man speak so fancy to me before. Once a fellow at a dance who'd had too much to drink told me I was, "a great looking dame," and men had certainly said fresh things to me when making passes, but most men had to have something to drink before they could get brave enough even to approach me. Mandy said I scared them off, but I don't know why.

And then, during the war they were either gone, or when they came back they seemed gripped by a frenzy to get married, an idea that always chilled me. The life of my mother, or my sister, was not what I wanted. Sometimes I scared myself. I knew I didn't want to lose my freedom. But it was all confused with the feelings that at times nearly overcame me. At least David seemed safe.

He turned back to the roses. He was relaxed, and with a silent sigh of relief, I relaxed too. Together we planted the roses. Maybe they're still there. They took hold right away and by the end of September were blooming so much that David cut some to take to his wife.

8. IF YOU WANT ME...

After that I was usually outside when he passed. As the summer took hold, David lost the routine of winter. Often he stopped to pass the time of day. Those were times of complete happiness for me. I took lots of walks on the beach, collecting the shells left behind by the waves. It became an obsession to see what new things were there. I found and kept so many that I felt guilty being so greedy. I wrote Mandy to tell the kids that I was collecting shells for them. It sounded so good I believed it myself.

More often than not, as I walked farther and farther I "happened" upon David. His favorite place was near a stump far up the beach. From that angle, early in the morning, the sunshine played on the Rock so that parts were in shadow.

He didn't just paint the Rock, he painted everything: the sea at storm, the seals, the gulls, many different places along the shore. He got tangled up in the colors, too, like me and my quilt. It was his fascination with the different shades of sand, and the different light--morning light and afternoon light, cloud light and sun light, shadows, rain drops and the bird footprints that added the depth to my quilt that it finally had. I've never looked at sand the same since.

And people. Sometimes he went to town or back in the hills to the farms. David knew most of the people who lived up in the mountains.

The Hosmer family lived up one of those dirt roads. About once a week David visited them, liking to have lunch with them but more, he loved seeing the children as they were, natural, so he could paint them later. He didn't want them posed, he watched them as they worked around the farm and did quick sketches that he finished in the winter. There was the Hosmer dad, and mother, and five kids. Three boys and two girls. Funny I should think of that now.

My favorite painting of his--oh, the mother's mother lived with them too--was one of the girls picking raspberries in their little patch with the grandma. The girl was about six. She had a little pail with a wire handle on it like her grandma's. Her face, in the picture, raspberry juice on her lips, and the most self-satisfied smile. A comfortable thing she was there, in the patch with her grandma. All to herself. The grandma had white hair that was kinda twirly 'round her head. She wore a flowered dress, and boots, and her berry pail hooked onto the old leather belt she had around her waist. She's looking into the bush and reaching to get a berry from the middle.

I loved that picture. It was inside their front door and sometimes I'd look at it and I'd be the grandma, and sometimes I'd be the little girl. It was cool in the bush and hot on our heads. David was good at faces, though he didn't think so.

Down by the water one day I was looking for more sand dollars to use as models for my quilt. But I was picking up everything else that wasn't broke when I saw David waving at me to come over. My apron was full of the shells so I walked rather than ran over to him like I wanted to.

The sand underfoot was white and dry. It squeaked as I crossed it. Gulls and crows were flying up and down the beach, looking to be more playing than seriously hunting for food. When I got to David he untied my apron so I could put the shells down. His face was a sight. His nose was sunburned and peeling. His reddish hair was windblown and sticking up every which way. To me he was the prettiest thing on the beach.

Something had him excited. After taking off my apron he
lifted me up on a stump and with his arm around my waist to
steady me, he pointed out to sea. I was more aware of his closeness
and his hand at my waist than of where he was pointing, but as I
looked I saw what he was so excited about.

There were three whales playing in the ocean, big, long gray
things. The calm sea allowed us see them more clearly than was
usual, plus they were closer than the ones I was used to seeing
from my window.

"I think those are called gray whales," David said, "Gosh,
aren't they grand?"

They were spouting and diving and looked to be having fun. It
made us both giggly. Maybe being so close together had something
to do with it, too. He had to hold me tight to keep me from falling,
and finally I had to get off the stump before I fell off it.

We sat down in the warm sand. As we talked he played with
it, piling it into mounds, then smoothing them flat. Dribbling
handfuls of sand, he made designs while asking me about the shells
I'd gathered.

"You have so many, going into business or something?" Did
he think I was greedy, or silly? I explained about my nieces and
nephews, and off-handedly told him about the quilt. He was
interested.

"But, David, the center is to be a piece-over of Haystack Rock,
and I've tried, and tried, and I can't copy it."

"Sophie, would you mind...?" His face was bright with an
idea, plus the sunburn. "One artist shouldn't interfere with
another..."

An artist? Me? I would have laughed, but he was so serious I
just smiled. "But we can help one another. What if I draw it for
you?"

I didn't expect his help. "Oh David, you shouldn't waste your time."

His blue eyes were earnest, "I'd like very much to do it."

"Okay. If you insist. I'd really like some help," I said. I'll admit that I wanted more than just his help. I wanted the drawing, yes, but because he would be thinking of me while he did it. To know that David was thinking just of me and doing something just for me was a pleasure I wanted very much.

Plus I was flattered. The family always took my quilts for granted, or teased me about my eternal, infernal stitching, and complained about the little pieces that seemed to float into every nook and cranny of the house. And here David was calling me an artist.

He changed the subject. "So, Sophie, you make quilts, and plant roses. I'm learning more about you every day. Tell me, which of the brothers is your husband, and how long will you be here?"

Me, married to one of my brothers? The idea was so ridiculous and too, my nerves were just stretched thin. I hooted and laughed 'til I got a stitch in my side, thinking first of Willie and then Zack as a husband to me.

"What's so funny?" he kept asking.

I finally got control of myself. "I'm here to help the boys, cook and clean for them. They pay me a little from their wages and I get to live at the beach. I was tired of being with my sisters. Willie and Zack and I, we all three like it."

"I wondered... I'm glad. The older one seems so gruff and unlike you that I didn't like to think of you married to him. I see him sometimes outside when I pass by in the evening, and he's barely civil. I don't think he approves of me." His eyes twinkled. "And the younger one, he stopped and talked to me on the beach, last year, and seems to like my painting...but he's too young, too immature. So..." "I wondered." While he was discussing my brothers as husbands, my mind was on his wife. I didn't want him to speak of her, but maybe I'd made the same mistake he had.

"But you, David, you're married, aren't you?" I hoped he'd laugh too and tell me she was his sister, or his housekeeper, anything but his wife.

"Of course I'm married."

He didn't notice my disappointment. I swallowed it and kept smiling brightly at him, while I murmured, "How nice," or something polite.

"Amy and I've known each other all our lives. It seems we've always been married. It's been about twelve years now."

"But where is she?" I insisted. "I never see her." I wasn't happy with his tone in speaking of her. He didn't sound at all like a miserable husband.

"You haven't seen Amy because she seldom comes to the beach. She used to come often when we first moved here about seven years ago, but now she's satisfied to stay at home, reading and taking care.

"She writes. When she's not off selling my paintings for me, that is. That's where she is right now, in Salem. She left a week ago. I have a dealer there who sells for me. She delivers a few to him. She has a regular route she follows all around the state, visiting small galleries, and shops, and people she knows who are particularly interested in what I have to sell. She loves to travel. And she really has a knack for selling, which is good, because I hate it. Getting out, seeing all her old friends and meeting new people, it's good for her. Sometimes," he said quietly, "she's gone all summer."

"Then she's not...sickly?" I wasn't overjoyed at the idea of such a healthy, self-reliant woman.

"Sickly? No. Whatever gave you that idea?"

"Well, Zack saw her last summer here on the beach..." It embarrassed me to admit I'd been talking about him.

The sun went out of his face. "Oh, that. Yes, last summer she wasn't well. For a while." It seemed difficult for him and I wished I hadn't pried.

"We lost our baby." His face tightened. I tried to stop him.

"You needn't tell me."

He took a long breath. "Amy was about three months along and we were very happy. We'd waited so long, and had just about accepted that we wouldn't have children when she realized she was carrying a child. She was very careful... But I guess it wasn't meant to be. Losing the baby was very hard on her. More on her thinking than on her body."

He sat quietly for a while, playing with the sand. Gulls screeched from down by the water, fighting over a bit of something washed up in the tide. I couldn't think of what to say. Then he squashed the tower he'd built, "But, it's all right now. We still have time. I'm thirty-five and she's only thirty-three.

"On to a more cheerful subject. How big should my drawing be?"

I was glad to talk of anything else. The last thing I wanted to hear was how happy he and Amy were. I preferred to forget her. As for the quilt I wasn't sure what size the middle piece should be, so he said he'd draw up several sizes and I could choose which one

I liked best.

As I got up to leave he put his hand on my shoulder. "I often see you walking on the beach. Please stop by and talk to me again."

"But I don't want to bother you."

"Sophie! I love to talk with you. Your laugh makes me glad."

I smiled at that.

"And sometimes I just get lonely here by myself. Promise me you'll come again."

"If you want me..."

"I do."

For the next week I saw him on the beach every day, and armed with the invitation always found my way over to him. I limited my time with him and hated leaving, but I was skittish, afraid that if I stayed too long he would know what a dummy I was, or at least what a dummy I thought I was.

For up 'til then no one had ever talked to me, with me, or maybe even more important, listened to me. He wanted to know what I thought. What I thought about books he'd read, whether I ever went out and just looked at the stars at night? Did I believe in God? What was my family like? What did I think happened after a person dies? Did I think there would ever be another war?

Funny things: had I ever seen a ghost, and did I think people had more than one life? If I could travel, where would I go, and why? Did I want to get married and have children? What did I want to do with my life?

I wasn't used to so many questions, and certainly none about most of the things he thought about. I'd take the questions home with me, the strange and new ideas and thoughts spinning in my head, and work out my answers while I sewed and cleaned, or walked on the beach.

Next day I'd go back full of answers and questions of my own and we'd be off again, talking and laughing a mile a minute, until I pulled myself away, frightened by the pull he had upon me. David would always touch me somehow, lightly across my shoulders, fussing about to make sure I was settled comfortably on the sand, taking my hands to help me up when I was leaving. And once he insisted on helping me brush the sand from my skirt when I stood up, causing such a feeling in me that I ran away.

The feelings he raised in me! I was sucked into him,
completely absorbed in him, but, oddly, I also felt separate, unique.
With him I felt at peace. Alone, or away from him I was confused.

He's married, I kept reminding myself, but the pull just kept
getting stronger. Every day I would tell myself, Today I'm not
going down there, I'll stay at home. But then, he would pass by in
the morning and wave, and I'd decide, Well, just for a little while
this afternoon if I haven't got anything else to do. And the day
would go on forever, until I left the cabin, and went to him.

Every day I used the excuse of the drawings to go talk to him.
"Are they done yet?" I'd ask and for a couple weeks I waited,
wondering if he was really working on them or just a talker. You
know how lots of men are... And every day he'd say, "Just a little
bit more, almost done," until it got to be almost a joke for me to
tease him and him to pretend that he was working on a masterpiece
and I needed to wait for the, "magic of the muse," whatever that
meant.

The day it happened... One day, about a couple of weeks later,
after the boys had left for work, I was rummaging through my
scrap bag when I heard what I knew was his knock on the door,
what they used to call a shave-and-a-haircut-two-bits knock. I
jerked and scraps fell on the floor. I tidied my hair quickly in the
small mirror in my bedroom and tried to appear casual when I
opened the door.

He'd never come into the cabin before. He took some time to
look around. I let him wander and started coffee, just to have
something to do besides stare at him. The fire in the stove was low,
it didn't take much but a couple pieces of wood to get it up enough
to cook the coffee. He offered to help but I brushed off his offer, I
needed to do something with my hands.

My clearest memory of him is the way he looked that day. He
was wearing a blue shirt that set off his eyes and tan prettily. His
hair seemed more red, but as usual, it was wild on his head. If I
hadn't grabbed the coffeepot I'd have reached for his hair. I always
wanted to touch it, pat it, pull my fingers through it.

He walked around the room, then stopped in front of the window. "I like your view." He smacked his lips like he was disappointed. "I tried to get this cabin. This land."

I watched him taking in the view, until he turned his head quickly, the sunlight flashing off his hair. His eyes caught mine.

"Oh, really?" I said, just to keep him talking. I didn't care what he was saying. My hands moved to the stove so I could open it and stir the wood about, reaching to the box for another small piece to shove in.

"Un huh," he said, "but our landlady, Mrs. Hope, said she'd rather rent it out and have some income than sell it and probably waste the money. The land our house is on was hers, too, but she wasn't making anything on it. She was glad to get rid of it."

He came to the shelf Zack had put up for me. I'd put my shells on it, and other doo-dads, just stuff I'd found. Now they took on a glow as he admired and fingered the trinkets with his easy hands. He had his back to me when he said, "How's the quilt coming along?" He whirled around to pull some sheets of paper out of his back pocket.

The drawings. In the excitement I'd forgotten them.

"Oh, David. Let me see!" I took the papers to the window and looked at each one, comparing them to the original, the Rock. They all seemed perfect to me. Then I remembered the scraps in my bag. Were any of them large enough? The reddish-brown from my good dress maybe? Leaving the papers on the windowsill and without even thinking of David, I went to my bedroom closet. I had the dress on the bed when David's hand touched me on the shoulder. "I guess you like them? Do I get a thank you?"

I whirled around and straightened up quickly. I was face to face with him.

"What? I am sorry. I didn't mean to startle you." He didn't step back.

His breath was warm on my face. His hand reached up to my hair, smoothed down to stroke my face.

My hands went to his hair. I was rigid, but my whole body felt alive, pushing towards him. In a last second questioning of myself I pulled back, but he looked at me and pulled me to him, easy.

"Relax," he whispered, "I won't hurt you." His kiss was like velvet, soft and warm, but strong, too. I had the strangest feeling, like I was melting into him. He unbuttoned my dress while I kissed his face. I felt the stubble of whiskers on my lips. I opened his shirt while his hands moved over my body.

By the time we were down to nothing I didn't want to stop him, or myself. He kept whispering, "So beautiful, so beautiful," as we lay together on my small bed, the brown dress among the heap of clothing on the floor.

I don't know how it was for you, Annie, your first time. I'd heard that a virgin is supposed to feel pain, but I didn't feel any. Only joy, and, afterwards, contented and wrung out. No remorse. That David loved me as completely as I loved him, I never had a doubt.

As we lay easy against each other I was at total peace but I felt a tremor startle him. "Oh, Sophie, dear, I hope you don't think when I said to thank me that I meant--"

"Well, no, but now that you mention it..." I shoved him over the side of the bed and he landed on the floor with a heavy thump.

"Sophie!" he yelled in a hurt tone as I laughed. His dignity and sense of humor sometimes clashed. When I'd do something a little rough or laugh at him when he wanted to be serious, his nose would get out of joint. A little kiss always smoothed him down. Sometimes I'd catch a wary look in his eyes when he got serious and, he'd warn me, "Now, So? Don't get mischievous." It was more fun to keep him just a little off-guard because, in too many things, he had the drop on me.

9. LIKE A GIRL IN LOVE...

That David loved me but that he also loved his wife was a fact I had to accept. It was never my intention to try to take him away from her. My desire was to have part of him for myself. We made each other happy, that was all I cared for.

We loved together many times that summer. Often the cabin was our place, but once, on a gray, foggy day he made love to me behind a barrier of driftwood. The open air with the cloak and damp of the day only added to my desire for him.

At home I tried to be as I'd always been.

My brothers were suspicious. I'd been seen walking on the beach with David. I was happy and cheerful around the house, which was always clean. The flowerbed was bright and the vegetable garden came up well. This efficiency bothered Zack.

I was setting the table one evening and singing, when he demanded, "Sophie, what's the matter with you?"

"Why, Zack," I answered innocently, "nothing's the matter with me. Don't you like my singing?"

"Stop acting so damn prissy. It ain't normal. Not for you it ain't."

Instantly I was on my guard. "What's so un-normal about singing?"

"It ain't the singing. It's the way you do it. Flouncing around here. Cleaning up all the time."

Willie got into it then. "Oh, leave her alone, Zack. She's just happy. Nothin' wrong with that."

"I'm not so sure. What's she got to be so happy about? Living here on this lonely beach doing our washing and cleaning? Is that enough to make a woman sing? I don't remember our mother singing and working."

Neither Willie nor I answered him. I was hoping the whole thing would blow over before Zack thought anymore. Then, slyly, he slipped it in, "You act like a girl in love."

I couldn't deny it, but I wasn't about to admit it either. I tried to divert him. "Sure, Zack, I'm in love. With cooking your stupid meals and washing your stinking clothes. And I just love the thanks I get. Do you ever appreciate it? No, all you do is complain about the lousy five bucks a week I keep."

It worked. At the mention of the five dollars he jumped up, shouting, "It's more than five bucks, missy. You take a 'wage' of two bucks a week, then get a buck-fifty apiece from us each week and then grab another three bucks apiece for us. For savings, supposedly. How do we know what you're doing with it?"

"Wait a minute, Zack!" Willie decided to defend me. "That's for our own good."

"I don't like it," Zack said, "It's my money and I never see it." While they argued I got the box with the bags from my bedroom. I'd started out with envelopes but that hadn't worked for very long as the cash started to pile up. So I made up three different bags for the money. I loved the feel and the sound of the money rustling around in the bags when I pulled the box from under my bed.

Willie's voice was loud. "You know we'd just blow it if she

didn't keep it for us." I came back and handed them their bags. Zack dumped his on the table and counted it. Ninety-six dollars. Not a great sum nowadays but a comfortable amount for then.

Willie handed me back his bag. He didn't even open it. "I want you to still keep it for me, Sophie. If you don't, I'll just waste it. I'll be going home in a month and if Nettie will have me, I want to marry her."

I knew Nettie, a girl who went to school with Willie, and I hoped, for his sake, that she would marry him. She came from a farm nearby where we bought pigs every spring to fatten and slaughter for winter.

She was prettier than any other girl around and was in a couple plays in school. I remembered especially once when we were over there and she took me into the house to show me the quilt she was working on. She had told me she'd like to join up with some people in Portland she knew about who put on real plays.

I also knew that she did like Willie, better'n he knew, but I wondered about her, could she be a good wife to him? Recalling that day at her place I didn't remember any big statements from her about how she was looking forward to settling down and cooking and cleaning for someone for the rest of her life. She made an impression on me because I'd had those thoughts, but she was the first other girl I knew who actually talked about doing something else. I couldn't see how she would really do what she talked about so I figured it wasn't something I needed to bring Willie's attention to. She was a good girl and I supposed she'd get over that stuff if she married Willie. So I kept my mouth shut and my doubts to myself.

"Sure, Willie," I agreed, "she'll like you even better for having money to get started." I knew that was true. She'd also said she didn't want to be a poor farmer's wife, which could mean that she was willing to be a well-off farmer's wife. I truly didn't know.

Zack shoved the money in his pocket and threw the bag down on the floor, then he picked it back up. "I been needing something to put my shoe stuff in. I'll just take this after all."

Things were all calmed down and we were eating dinner and Zack was planning the good time he'd have with his money, the girls he'd dance and romance, when he remembered.

"Who could the guy be?"

"What guy?" Willie said. If he'd had any sense he'd have kept quiet, but he was too busy eating meatloaf and boiled taters to be thinking.

"The guy Sophie's goofy over." He put his fork down and looked at me. "You haven't been to a dance in...since Spring sometime." He nodded his head as he calculated time, moving his lips as he brought his focus on me. I felt a coldness along my spine and, touching the bowl of potatoes said to Willie, "Oh, I got a little bit of butter made today." He didn't even hear me. Zack had his attention.

"Aw, that don't mean nothin' Zack, Sophie's just too nice a girl for those roughnecks."

"Yeah?" He shook his head. "I'll take that butter." He smirked at Willie. "They weren't too rough for her before." A heat of anger and fear surged through me. I jumped up and grabbed the butter from the cooling shelf and slammed it down on the table beside Zack's plate. I wanted to slam him on the head with it but I'd worked too hard to ruin the butter. He didn't seem to notice my anger except for the smirk getting bigger on his face.

"Out with it Sophie girl, who is it?"

This time I was determined to stop it but it was beyond me. Standing over by the stove cleaning up the cooking mess I said, as casually as I could, seeing as I was blood-red mad, "There's nobody, Zack. It's just like Willie said, none of your pals are the kind of men I truly choose to be spending time with."

He looked at me then, and mimicked, "'Truly choose?'" and then slid into his regular voice, "Huh! It's my bet someone is feathering your nest right here. The hen don't have to wander far when she's got a rooster right close to home."

Both Willie and I stared at him, me because he had me nailed to the wall. I tried to distract him, "That's what I mean, crude talking like that. That's all you know, you and your pals."

"Smithers?" Willie cut right through it. "You don't mean Smithers?" He stared at Zack who just shook his head at Willie like he was a simpleton.

"Of course I mean Smithers. Who else is around here? Not the rough guys we work with. Oh no, it's that Fancy Dan with the smooth hands. I'll bet he's smooth everywhere else too, eh, Sophie." He leered at me.

I felt my face go crimson. The fire was hot in me. "Don't talk to me like that."

Willie jumped up, outraged. "That's enough, Zack! Sophie's our sister, and Smithers is a married man. So they like to talk, that's no reason to get foul-mouthed about it. I know Smithers and he's decent. One more word like that and I leave. And Sophie goes with me."

That startled me. I kept silent but I had no intention of going anywhere. Willie's threat immediately calmed Zack down. Without me he'd be back to taking care of himself. He didn't want to do that.

"For God sakes, Willie, I was only kidding. Don't you know nothing? Sit down, eat your supper. Forget I said anything." He took up the butter and started spreading some on his potatoes.

Willie looked at him and then at me.

I shrugged my shoulders, like what could we do with Zeke, and motioned him to sit down at the table again. "Forget it, Willie. Finish your dinner. I've also got some pie tonight." He looked at me again. For one horrid moment I thought he was going to question me about David, then he shrugged and sat back down.

"What kind of pie?" He was so serious it would have made me laugh if I wasn't so frightened. I showed him the salal berry pie that I'd made in the cool of the morning with berries I'd picked the day before with David. He tucked into his dinner, a smile on his face.

We finished our meal in silence, but Willie's words had been like a bucket of cold water thrown onto a forest fire. They didn't put out the flame I felt for David but I was more in control now. Willie was right.

David was a married man. And I was beginning to suspect I was a pregnant woman. I felt disaster just around the corner. I was two weeks past my monthly, not usual for me. In another three weeks I'd know for sure.

10. WHAT AM I GOING TO DO...?

My mind was clear, I must tell David. If I was pregnant I was no more than a month along. Maybe he would know what to do. Having a baby out-of-wedlock in those days was unthinkable. Shameful. I was terrified at the possibility.

The day after the argument I went to the beach. I found him near our log. He was happy to see me and hugged me hard and kissed me right there in the open. I hardly cared. "David, we've got to talk."

He knew something was very wrong. "Sure, honey, what's the matter?"

We sat on the log and I plunged right in. "I think I'm pregnant."

I certainly didn't expect him to leap up, laughing, and then reach down, grab me and yell, "Tremendous!" right in my face, but that's what he did.

I was shocked, surprised. "But, David," I tried to say. He didn't hear me.

"Are you sure? Oh, honey. This is wonderful! How far?" At last he was going to listen to me.

"You act like this is a glorious event. It's not! You're a married man. What's going to happen to me?" I could feel tears starting but I swallowed them. "David, do you know anyway to stop it?"

He looked like I had struck him. "You just put that idea out of your head right now. You could die."

"David, you don't understand. What am I going to do?"

"Do?" He had the simplest explanation of all. "You'll come live with me, of course."

"With you? And what will Amy think of this fine idea?." I

thought he'd gone mad. Maybe he was "Crazy Smithers" after all.

"Why Amy thinks it's just fine."

"What do you mean Amy thinks it's just fine? She doesn't know about us, does she?"

He looked bewildered for a minute. "Sure, she knows. I couldn't keep something like this from her. She's known I love you since last spring, when we planted the roses."

All I could think was that David was off his rocker, and so was his wife.

"Look Sophie, maybe it does sound a little odd, but Amy and I... We don't believe a wedding band should cut you off from life. No one person can be everything to another. Amy loves the city, and plays, and crowded smoky rooms full of people. I hate it. So when she leaves in the summer she does all those things, with men who do enjoy them."

"Does she make love to them, like you do with me?" The whole idea was absurd, but I couldn't help asking. For a moment I ignored my predicament.

"No, she hasn't. It's just that it's her choice. So far she hasn't met any man she loves but me. But I'll understand if she does."

"But, David," I was repeating myself. "It's so dangerous. What if she finds someone, and leaves you?"

"Why ever should she leave me? The core of me is her and the core of her is me. That will never change. I know that as certainly as I know I love you and you love me. Do you doubt that I love you?"

"No." I didn't. I was absolutely certain.

"Okay. It's settled. Amy gets back the last week in September. We'll know for certain whether you're going to be a mother by then."

"David." It was time for some serious talking, of the way the world really is, not the way David wanted it to be. "This just won't work."

"Sure--"

"No, wait. You've got some starry-eyed notion that Amy is just going to be delighted to welcome me into her home. She's not. I'll bet everything I have on it, which isn't much. She may be all you say. If she has allowed you to go with me...knowing all about me...then she is, well, unusual. I certainly wouldn't have left you alone here with me."

For the first time he was concerned, "You're not a jealous woman, are you, Soph?"

That made me laugh, though it came out bitter. He was worried that I was a jealous woman. "Frankly, I've never had the chance to find out. I've never been in love, until you."

"How do you feel about Amy?"

Finally, I'd gotten to him. "I don't think about her. She's been gone all summer. It's like she doesn't exist. I never thought about living with her. I can't believe even now that you would ever consider it. Why, she'd have to be a saint to do that." Or nuts, I thought.

"The Mormons do it."

"What?"

"You know they do, and they get along all right. They don't think it's crazy."

"Maybe they don't but everybody else does." I was suddenly suspicious. "You're not a Mormon, are you?" That would explain his crazy ideas.

"No, I'm not. But we grew up in Utah, so I've heard stories."

Then I remembered what he'd told me about his growing up, and I was relieved, let me tell you. An odd religion thrown in would have baked the cake.

"This whole thing is too much for me. I'm getting a headache. Whatever happens I'm not moving into your house. It's just not right."

"I wouldn't force you to do something you think is wrong, but please, Sophie, at least think about it."

I promised to do that but I had no intention of giving in. I didn't want to meet Amy, nor even see her, let alone share her husband in the same house with her.

We parted without even a kiss. He tried but I wasn't feeling too well. I just wanted to go home, and lie down. He teased me then about being "...just like a wife with headaches and no lovin'."

I didn't see anything to laugh about. I waved him away and trudged off through the sand. As I walked up the path to the cabin, I thought how easy it would be to slip and fall, and lose the baby. Something else within me made me walk even more carefully, lest I fall and hurt the baby. I knew it was crazy thinking but if I was carrying a child, it was David's as well as mine, and he wouldn't want to lose another one.

When I got home I laid down for a while until I felt better.
Then I started thinking about Willie and Zack. The road job would
close down at the end of September, about the same time Amy
would be back. I still had no notion of living with them, but I
wanted to be close to David for as long as I could, no matter
whether I was pregnant or not. Willie would be going home to
Nettie--no problem there--but Zack was going to another
construction job, in California, and was expecting me to go with
him. I had to think of a believable reason for staying here in the
cabin.

Telling him I was "in trouble" was out of the question, but
what if I told him that Amy was pregnant and that David had asked
me if I could stay and help? No, not just help. If Zack thought I
could earn more money by staying rather than going with him... He
wouldn't like it, but he understood money.

She'd been gone since late June. She couldn't be less than three
months along. But did Zack know that most problems happen in
the first three months? I was sure he didn't. Even so, there were
other complications I could dream up.

After I got it satisfied in my mind that I could handle the boys,
I put my thoughts to David. I had best get to know him even better.
What did I really know about this man who might be the father of
my child, and who had such strange ideas?

11. IF HE ONLY KNEW...

*D*avid's father had been a Baptist minister in Virginia. When David was small his parents moved the family to Utah. Three families came with him from Virginia, all with equal purpose, to bring the True Word to the Mormon heathens. Their original goal had been Salt Lake City. Within a week of their arrival, Preacher Smithers and his small, fervent group found out that, "The Devil had those people caught tightly in his talons." Preacher Smithers decided the Lord was telling him that he hadn't meant Salt Lake City at all. Better to start small, perhaps some place where the Devil hadn't got such a firm hold.

Thus inspired they moved, hurriedly, as David remembered it, to a small town about fifty miles away.

They prayed and worked hard. After fifteen years the score was BAPTISTS: one. The Lutheran family changed to 'good Baptist Christians' because the Baptist church was convenient, and a possible two, being a Mormon woman who was friendly. MORMONS: everybody else, including David's brother who married a Mormon girl, becoming an LDS convert. David married Amy about that time. She being from the Lutheran family the Baptists figured they were at least even, but weren't sure.

Preacher Smithers was hearty in his approval of the marriage, considering the disaster that had befallen the eldest son. He encouraged David to move on to less soul-endangering surroundings. They feared the exposure of future grandchildren to the predominant religion. David would have left anyway, as he was filled with a longing for an ocean he'd never seen.

His success as a painter was slow, but he worked lumbering and part-time as a hired hand. They never starved, and David was content to remain by the sea for the rest of his life.

Their unusual ideas of life were a mixture of what they saw in their growing up, and from reading. David told me that there was more than one approach to life and marriage. He was determined not to get set in a mold. "It makes moldy people," he would later tell me.

He had a bit of the preacher in him, too. Not in religious ways, but he loved to talk, and could at times be most stubborn to have people agree with him. It was amazing to him that Amy didn't immediately grasp the truth of his ideas. "But, it's so clear!" he would shout.

That was always the end of the sermon, because Amy would say, "Amen, David." He would purse his lips in annoyance, but stop.

But David's strongest holdover from his father's influence was what he called his inability to swear properly. I first heard his expression, "Cotton pickin' thunderbolts," when he went to push a stick farther into a campfire and burned his hand on the fire in the coals. He dropped the stick and exploded with the oath.

I laughed. I'd expected "Damnation!" at least, and told him so.

"I've tried." Clearly, he was hurt at my laughter. "But it just doesn't work. I had it pressed in me hard as a youngster that only bad people swear. I never really believed it 'cause Amy's Dad seemed to get relief from a good "Damn!" now and then. Other than that, I just didn't hear much swearing where I grew up. But I was willing to learn. After Amy and I left home, I worked with a lumber crew and practiced everything I heard--not around Amy of course. But, you know, Sophie, something was wrong." His eyebrows wrinkled in bewilderment.

"Every damn came out sounding like darn and Hell! always
made me nervous. The worse ones were beyond me. They stuck in
my throat and sounded weak when they came out. The guys
laughed at me. They called me... oh, never mind."

I wanted to explore that, but he got red so I let it be.

"I gave it up and went back to my old home words. I decided
it's not what you say as much as how you say it. I get just as much
satisfaction from a good, hearty 'Cottinpickin'!' as Mr. Swenson
did from his 'Damn'."

I think it was David's only defeat, except for me, and I wasn't
a complete loss.

The next two weeks went on eternally. Every day after the
boys left for work, David would stop at the cabin. We would have
a cup of coffee and then go for a long walk on the beach or build a
fire and sit and talk. One thing we didn't do in that two weeks was
make love. I wanted to, he wanted to. But I stopped him, thinking,
if I maybe wasn't with child we should quit while we still had the
time. Suddenly the chances I had taken seemed so foolhardy. I
wasn't ignorant of the facts of life. But the passion I felt for David
had swept all caution from my mind. For two weeks, we didn't do
it.

We talked a lot, but David never said he was sorry for making
me pregnant, because he wasn't. He hoped I was.

And I hoped I wasn't.

My monthly never came and my breasts got tender, and I
threw up in the morning, two days in a row. The second morning,
afterwards, I was sitting in front of the cabin on the bench Willie
had made. I was being still, breathing in the cool of the morning,
watching the fog lift over the sea, when David came down from his
place and sat on the bench beside me. Zack and Willie had gone to
work hours before, so we were completely alone. Except I wasn't
feeling alone. I knew I was growing a child within me.

I was happy to see David, I needed his comforting hands holding mine. And his words. "Hey, sweet." He glanced at me with worried eyes. "What's up? Wanna walk?"

"In a minute." I shifted on the bench to face him, my view changing to the length of the beach. In the distance I could see a family of Mom, Dad, dog, and three children going toward the waves, the kids kicking at the sand, the dog leaping around them all.

"I wonder, David, with all your smarts, is this baby a boy? Or a girl?" I watched his face.

His white teeth showed as he grinned widely. I remember that moment so clearly. He swallowed, hard. I reached out and touched his Adam's apple, just a light stroke. He took my hand and put my fingers to his mouth, kissed them.

"Oh, a boy would be nice this time, or a girl, one or the other. You choose." He leaned his head back and closed his mouth, just laughing from deep inside.

I snuggled into him, not caring who might see.

He put his arm around me. "Wanna walk?"

"Yes, indeed. We've been waiting for you." I felt full to bursting over, full of energy and love and a need to move.

He jumped off the bench. My end flew up so I started to fall. He caught me, pulled me up straight, and dropped my hands, grinning.

"Race you!" he shouted, then remembering my condition, fell back. "Oh, I guess not."

I took my chance, dashed past him, down the path, not running full tilt but keeping ahead of him.

"Not fair," I heard him say through running breaths.

"I never said I was fair." I got to the water first. He let me to be sure, but I enjoyed my triumph. For just a minute he took my hand and we walked that way a few feet before he remembered my need for caution in public and let it go. I just sighed, confused with both happiness and sadness. For that morning, happiness won out.

David had enough sense not to dance around when we were sure. He was just quietly happy. The corners of his mouth would twitch with a held-back grin when he looked at me. He took to patting my belly and breasts in a pleased and protective way. At first it annoyed me, but his joy was catching. And I was never one to mope for long about something I could do nothing about.

The last week before Amy came home we made our plan. David arranged with the landlady for me to continue to rent the cabin. He told her that I would be staying to help with his wife. I told the same story to Zack and Willie. I don't think Zack believed it, but he kept his thoughts to himself. He didn't care what happened to me as long as he wasn't around to be shamed. He left for California a week before Willie was to go home.

Willie was outside when Zack was leaving. He turned to me at the door and said, nastily, "I do hope you've had fun." He looked from my face to my belly, and left.

It shook me. I was afraid he'd say something to Willie, but when Willie came back he was all smiles as usual. That was on Sunday.

Wednesday morning David stopped for his coffee. He asked how the quilt was coming along. I knew it was an excuse to get into my bedroom. I hadn't worked much on the quilt for the last three weeks. I pulled him behind the curtain where he took me gently in his arms. "Soph?" he said.

"Yes, please." His touch on my back was a welcome fire.

We lay down on the bed, close together. He was leaning over me, kissing me, with his hand stroking my belly when the curtain flew back. There was Willie, a look of murder on his face. I think if he'd actually caught us making love he'd'a killed us both.

61

"So, Zack was right!" he yelled. Before we could move he'd pulled David off the bed and flung him on the floor like a feather. He stood for a second staring at me.

I was so scared.

"You're no better'n a whore."

David wasn't a fighter. That wasn't his way, but at that moment he'd have killed Willie or died trying, before he let me be harmed. He jumped up, both his hands flexing, balling into fists and flattening out in front of him at Willie.

"Get out of here!" The words snapped from him to Willie with the force of a whip. His cold anger shocked Willie.

It stopped him long enough for me to roll off the bed and at least die standing up. I thought of rolling under the bed, but as much as I longed for a rock to crawl under, I feared David was in danger of being beaten to death by my strong ox of a little brother. I dodged past them and ran into Willie's room where I got his deer rifle, which he always kept loaded.

When I got back David was on the floor , blood streaming from his nose. Willie raised his boot and I knew for certain he'd stomp him to death.

I pointed the gun straight at Willie. "You touch him again and I'll shoot you right now."

Willie stopped his boot in midair. I meant it, and he knew it.

David knew it, too. He staggered up.

"For God's sake, Sophie!" David almost fell into me. "Don't! Don't shoot!" His voice was rough, raw, almost like crying. I knew he was afraid I'd do it before he could stop me.

All the fight went out of Willie. His face twisted as he pulled in his anger. He turned away from us, ripped roughly at the bedroom curtain and pushed through to stumble to the kitchen table. He jerked out chair a and almost fell into it.

He was crying. "I don't understand, I don't understand."

David reached outward and put a hand on his shoulder. "Willie, Sophie and I love each other."

Willie's shoulder jerked to throw off David's hand. "Love!" He spat out. He made it sound like a dirty word. "A married man loves his wife."

He turned, glaring, to me. "And to think I stood up for you when Zack had it figgered out all along. If he only knew."

Willie and I had always been close, it shattered me to hear him talk like that. The mention of Zack was like sea water on a fresh wound. I didn't care what Zack thought of me, but I knew I could never go home again if Willie told Mom and Dad, or anybody in the family. There'd be no way to ever explain David and me. None of the sisters would have ever trusted me with their husbands again, though they needn't have worried. In the Elms, no one played around with married people.

As for the baby, I'd already cooked up a story about a quick romance with a fisherman after Willie left. After a mythical wedding, and the baby had come, my husband would conveniently drown in a storm on a fishing boat. It was a wild idea, and now I realize, very thin, but it was the only chance I had of saving any face at all. The baby would have to be explained, sooner or later, but I didn't intend for it to be this way.

"Willie, you must never tell Zeke. You must never tell anybody. They'd never understand. They'd hate me. You know it."

I must have got to him with the wildness of my appeal. He glared at me for a long time. "Okay, Sophie. But it's the last favor I ever do for you." Abruptly, he stood up.

David put a protective arm around my shoulders.

"You needn't worry," Willie said, the fight gone from him.

"I'm through with the both of you. I'm going home."

He went to his room and threw everything he owned into his old bag. Before he went out the door, I handed the moneybag of his savings to him. He looked at it queerly, then took the money out and stuffed it into his old bag. He dropped the empty bag onto the floor.

"I forgot my lunch," he said, and then went out, closing the door firmly behind him.

"Forgot his lunch? Whatever did...?"

David pointed to Willie's lunch pail, still on the table where I set it for him every morning. We hadn't even noticed it.

12. BUT, IT'S ALL ARRANGED...

*M*aybe it was my condition. After Willie left the tears started. I cried 'til I thought my heart would crack or my guts fall out. It hurt. All the fear I'd held bottled up came out in one great gush. Something dried up in me that day. Only one more time was I to cry so deeply, and even then...

After it was done, I was drained, like a stone, cold and lifeless. If anything was going to shake out that baby that day ought to have done it. But, thank God, it didn't.

David worried about me. For the next few days, he coddled me like a beloved sick child, bringing me tea with honey in it, cooking soup, trying to make me laugh. Finally, somehow, I came back to life again, to myself. It was impossible, with David around, to stay gloomy too long. He was like life itself, always positive that things would turn out for the best.

He stayed at the cabin until it was time to go pick up Amy. I dreaded his leaving, afraid I'd never see him again. I knew if I was Amy and he suggested to me what he was about to suggest to her, that my reaction would be to get him away from there as fast as I could, or demand that I go. Knowing that Amy's hold on him was longer and stronger than mine, she just might be able separate us.

That's one of the reasons I told him I would not agree to live with him and Amy. If she was half the woman David said she was, she just might be able to put up with me at a distance, unseen. The truth? I couldn't imagine facing her. Willie's reaction had been so severe against me, and he was my own flesh and blood. What might hers be?

Amy held all the cards. With one word she could stop David in his happy tracks, and destroy me as well. She had only to say No, for I wouldn't fight for him. If he'd ever given the slightest hint that he was unhappy with Amy, I would have. But he never suggested leaving her. It never even occurred to him. It was more than the fact that that people seldom got divorced in those days; she was part of him. They were like the alternating threads in a piece of fabric, together they made a whole. If I had tried to replace her I'd have had to unwind them first and it would have weakened David. I loved him too much for that.

During the time David stayed with me I managed to undermine his confidence in his happy plan enough to squelch some of his so-obvious glee. It annoyed the hell out of me that he was so fearless, and it seemed to me, unrealistic. Thus, when he left, he at least had some fear of Amy's reaction.

I don't think I slept a wink all night. I walked the floor, and drank coffee. For a while the slice of moon lit the surf. Then clouds moved in and the moon slid on down the sky, making the night even darker. I was grateful for the dawn, so I could give up the pretense of sleeping. I made oatmeal and toast for breakfast and only nibbled the toast. I made bread more for the work of it, to have something to do, than because I needed it. I pounded and kneaded that dough until all the air bubbles were popped and the surface was shiny. Might have been the best bread I ever made.

By the afternoon I was certain I'd never see David again. My palms were sweaty, my heart feeling heavy in my chest. I could feel it pounding. With every outside noise I went to the door and opened it, until I gave up and settled at the kitchen table. The bread had risen and baked and I'd even eaten a piece of it. I watched the waves surge in and out, the surf breaking with the white foam against the gray of the autumn ocean. I sat with my hands in my lap, not trying to busy them or my mind. Waiting.

I was watching the clouds lighten as the sun set behind them when I heard David's knock on the door. My hands flew up and settled again in my lap before I was able to say, "Come in, David."

He came in all smiles. His first words were, "Are you ready?"

Ready for what: to be shot? Killed? Maimed in some horrible way by an outraged wife? I was too stunned to speak.

He must have realized he'd been abrupt. He put his arms around me, lifting me to stand with my head on his shoulder. "Everything's all right. I told you it would be."

I couldn't believe it, "Come on, she wants to meet you."

At that, I pulled back. "Never."

"Don't be silly, how are you going to live with us without ever meeting Amy?" He thought he had everything solved because he had been able to get one woman to agree to his crazy scheme.

I was suddenly so weary that I had to sit down. He was looking around like he was deciding what I should bring with me.

"I told you before that I wouldn't live with you."

His forehead wrinkled and his eyes grew wide. "But Sophie, it's all arranged. Amy agrees with me, I'll fix it with the landlady."

"Don't 'But Sophie' me. To have Amy agree to me even being in the same country with you is enough for me. I don't want to meet her, I couldn't face her. And I doubt--"

"You're getting upset for--"

"--that she really wants to meet me."

He couldn't budge me. He finally had to accept it. That's the way it stayed for the next five months.

13. A BIT OF FLUFF

David visited every day. Amy sent books for me to read, though I wasn't much of a reader. Once in a while she sent soup and bread, which I ate because David saw to it that I did. He and I went for walks when the weather wasn't too stormy, me all bundled up like a mummy.

I was uncomfortable outdoors. Amy had the advantage of being able to see me, to watch me through that telescope. David insisted she wasn't watching me, but I knew she could if she wanted to. I would have.

The first month being alone wasn't so bad. October, a wonderful month along the coast. But as winter set in, and dragged on--oh, the loneliness. It got terrible. The rain wasn't too bad, at least it was something to watch, but the ever lastin' fog beat me.

It curled up and settled around the cabin, at first like a cozy blanket. After a while it became like a prison. Nothing but gray ever which way I looked. The continual roaring of the winter ocean got on my nerves. When the big storms came, the waves smacked against each other with a loud CRACK! then thundered down on the sand. It was exhilarating when there was someone to share it with; alone it frightened me. Even with no storm there was always that noise of the water moving. I began to understand why Amy didn't go down anymore.

When David was with me I didn't hear the ocean and it didn't matter what the weather was. He came for lunch every day, bringing groceries and newspapers and gossip from town. The two hours he stayed became the only part of the day worth getting up for.

The thing that saved my sanity, I'm sure, was the company of Punkin Sue Tiger, a golden kitten David gave me for Halloween. He came late one afternoon, near evening, his hands behind his back. "Close your eyes and put out your hands," he said.

I didn't feel comfortable doing that since one of my brothers handed me a snake once. After he promised I would like the surprise, I yielded, as I did in so many things to him.

The moment David put a little warm bundle of fur into my hands, my eyes snapped open. It was the cutest thing--a furry kitten, about six weeks old. He squeaked when I lifted him up close, then started purring when I laid him on my shoulder. The more I petted him the louder his purrs got. Like David's grin, Punkin Sue Tiger's purring captured my heart.

After David left, the kitten followed me around the cabin. I warmed up a bit of milk and put it in front of him but he only drank a little before, with tiny mews, he was exploring the cabin again.

I named him Punkin Sue Tiger because of his color and the fact we didn't know what sex he was. We thought he was a she, thus Sue, after a particularly catty woman I knew up home.

In the evening I sat in the chair looking out the window at the ocean. Punkin Sue Tiger came up and began playing at my bare toes, trying to grab them as I rocked. He made more happy little mews as I picked him up to avoid the rocker's legs, he settled right down on my lap as I stroked his golden fur. Mixed in with the pumpkin color were a few darker, tiger stripes. His little body just vibrated while I petted him.

I pulled lightly on his tail, he turned around and looked at me in such a way that I stopped, but then I just couldn't help myself, I

did it again. This time that little thing growled at me. Like most
guys he didn't much like me to laugh at him, but he wasn't serious
enough about it to get off my lap.

When I went to bed I put him in a box padded with rags, but
after a couple of meows I got up and put him on the cover beside
me, the top quilt edge turned back over him to keep him warm.

When I woke up he was still beside me, but snuggled under
the covers, his whiskers tickling at my chin. His bright eyes were
staring at me, his little mouth was open, crying at me to get up. He
was too small to get off the bed without falling. I took him outside
with me for his morning walk and he seemed as happy to get back
in the warm house as I was.

He delighted me. He was something to talk to, and play with,
and care about. And he gave me no complicated arguments.

I did spoil him terrible so that he crawled up the chair and
hung around my neck like a fox fur when I was sewing, or once in
a great while, when I was reading a paper. The rattle of the paper
teased him like a mouse and he'd swipe at it with his tiny claws.
Later, he got to be a real nuisance with the embroidery thread but
no matter what he did, he kept me from suffering more.

14. THE QUILT AND A LETTER

*W*ithout the boys to do for I had a lot of time on my hands. I took over their room for sleeping, turned mine into a sewing place and took back up with the quilt.

David helped with more drawings of patterns for the rocks. He had strong ideas about the colors I should use. Even wanted to bring me some blue material Amy had that he said would be just right for the water where it met the sky, but I wasn't having any of her material in my quilt. It was our quilt, I didn't want any of her in it.

From a sheet Willie had left behind, I made a new bag into which I would put all the material to go into Beach. I lugged my old bag of rags into the front room, where the fire warmed me and the light from the window brightened my dark mood. Bringing out all the old materials brought up the past, everything seemed so simple then, now my life was a tangle. The ocean moved slowly in large swells. Sometimes I would just sit and stare at it, watching the birds flying in and out of the thin fog, then I'd go back to sorting material.

I usually made pieced quilts, Beach was an appliqué, you know, small pieces sewn onto to a larger piece to make a design. It was the first one I ever did that way. Even with David's help, I still frustrated myself over the colors. There were the brown and gray leftovers from Zack's quilt, and some blue. More of Zack ended up in Beach than I planned, but as I worked on the quilt I forgot the bad things and only remembered that first night when he went poetic on us. So what had been a bad memory eased into pleasant.

I used large chunks of gray from a wool army blanket that he'd got from somebody who brought it back from the war. It was darker than I liked, but what the heck. The Army hadn't asked me before dyeing their blankets. It would do well for the frame around the front piece.

I separated out the rich light blue of a cotton blanket I'd used for Zack's border and as a runner between the squares. I loved the color, which reminded me of the eyes of a Siamese cat. Of course it didn't have the see-through quality of a cat's eye, but it was a lovely shade of blue. There was a lot of it. I'd only cut from the sides leaving me about half a blanket, good for the deeper ocean behind the rocks. I'd have liked more. Greedy? I made do with what I had. There was even some left over that I used in the Name Quilt.

The leftovers from Willie were fewer and smaller, but that was okay, because so much of Beach was drab grays and deeper blues. The little spots of color stood out and brightened it in a way that a fully-colored design wouldn't have.

For the lighthouse I found an especially clear emerald green, perfect for the sea around the base. I think it was left over from the collar of a cousin's flower girl dress. Yellow came from a piece I'd bought special for a quilted pillow I made for Mandy's wedding present--it fit for the lighthouse beam--just a tiny spot but a memory of comfort for me every time I saw it.

So many other bits of color I'd scavenged from aprons I'd made for Christmas presents for Mom and my sisters over the years. Tiring of pulling them out piece by piece, I upended the bag onto the floor. I didn't have much money but I was rich in material. Calicos and stripes and prints along with plain blacks, blues, and greens. Not much extra yellow because I used it so much in my quilts. Every bit of fabric took me back to what now seemed like an easier time.

I pulled out a bright orangish-yellow from the skirt I'd made
for Mandy when she was pregnant with one of the first kids. She
never liked it, so was happy to donate it to my quilt bag when I'd
packed to go to the beach with the boys. That seemed so long ago.
The orange was perfect for the starfish clinging to the rocks at the
base of Haystack.

I smoothed the orange material flat, my heart filling with a
bittersweet feeling. I'd used that color in every one of the stars in
Willie's quilt, with a narrow band of it around the outside for a
frame. It was so cheerful. It had taken a lot of piecing because I'd
cut it sparingly, not wasting one scrap.

The pieces laid in a heap while I stared out at the ocean,
seeing the tide line and the little birds skittering along the edge
picking up broken bits of clam or tiny bits of fish. If I was close up
I would hear their little cheeps sounding like baby chicks calling to
their mother.

I got on with the job, tossing back into the old bag the
patterned material leaving only the plain for the front of the quilt.

Every day I pulled the Beach bag into the front room and
settled myself into the chair between the table and the window. It
took days to get the pieces cut just right. And more weeks to get
them pinned onto the large curtain piece David bought new from
Puffin, a large plain piece of cotton but of substantial strength to
hold the appliqué.

The day he brought it he also carried with him a letter. I saw it
poking out from his jacket but was excited about the cloth, and
planning how I'd dye it a pale blue as backdrop for the sea and sky.
I didn't know the letter was for me. I made us tea while we talked
about how to use the cloth when suddenly he slapped his forehead
with the palm of his hand.

"Oh, I forgot. When I picked up the material today from
Puffin he gave me this letter for you."

He handed it to me and I was staring at my name written in
Mandy's big scrawly handwriting on the front. I felt the letter and

held it up to the light from the window and rubbed it and flattened it. It was pretty thin.

"Guess she doesn't have much to say," I said and put the envelope on the table.

"Aren't you going to open it?"

"Well, sure. But I thought we could drink our tea first."

"Sophie. How long has it been since you heard from your family?"

"Well, that's kind of just it. Maybe I don't want to. Maybe Zack or Willie told them something about, well, you know. Us.

Maybe my brothers told my mother about you and me. Maybe Mama has figured out that I'm not just staying as a housekeeper for the neighbors."

"If you don't open it you'll never know."

"Maybe I'd rather not know." He was always pushing at me.

"Okay, Sophie. I've got to get back to the house. I'd sure be interested to know what your sister has to say, when you finally read it. You will open it, won't you?"

"Uh huh." I picked up the cotton material and started folding it.

He left and I messed around with the pieces that I'd cut out with David's design, opening the curtain material back up and trying pieces on it to see how'd they look. I'd still have to wash and iron it, and dye it, but I needed to try it out first. I pinned Haystack Rock just to the left of center, a bit below the halfway mark so there'd be room for the tide pools. Haystack was a perfect reddish brown, like it is when the sunset turns the sky red. The two thumbs out of the same cloth went to either side. At the place of the tide pools I pinned on the smaller rocks and attached some of the starfish and anemones and pieces of tide pool plants. David had found a sand-colored piece onto which he'd drawn the little birds that skittered over the sand in that way they had that I loved. On another piece he'd drawn seagulls.

The letter sat on the end of the table where I'd pushed it to make room for the pieces. I forgot, almost, that it was there, until it started getting too dark for the close work I had to do. When I went to fold up the cloth to put it away the letter got knocked to the floor. I left it there while I put everything back in the sewing chest where Punkin Sue Tiger couldn't get at it.

I made another cup of tea and put another piece of wood in the stove and stirred the beans I was cooking for dinner. All the while thinking about every possible thing that Mandy could have to say, going back and forth from things the boys could have told her, to telling myself that the letter wouldn't have anything to do with me, to worrying that maybe something had happened to somebody in the family. Mama or Daddy? I finally sat down at the table with the letter and used my pocketknife to open it.

She didn't have the best handwriting but what she said was clear. She wanted to bring the kids down to the ocean. Would I have room for them in the cabin? She didn't have money to spare to rent a cabin but would bring enough of her canned food to help out while she was there and she'd thought from what I'd said in the letter I'd sent several months back that we could get clams and fish enough from the ocean that we'd all have enough to eat. Maybe we could make clam chowder?

Here? She was going to come here? I could barely breathe as I thought about it. I'll tell you, Annie, I never wrote a letter back to someone so fast in my life.

Of course most of it was a lie. It had to be. I couldn't tell her the truth.

I ate some beans and bread while I thought about what to say. Before I went to bed I'd written my letter, telling her that I was now living in the house with the Smither's family 'cause the wife needed me in the house. The cabin was rented out to another family and as much as I'd love to see them, this spring just wasn't going to be a good time because the wife would be having a baby sometime around then. I was going to be very busy and not able to visit. Maybe another time?

For once I was glad my family didn't have money for vacations and like that. I'm ashamed at how easy it was to lie to her and how easy it all came out of me that way. But, it worked. She wrote back saying she was sorry. The children had really been looking forward to it, which I thought was silly because they didn't know anything about the ocean and were still little enough to not care about going someplace. I figured that was Mandy's way of telling me how disappointed she was.

I was relieved. The day I got the first letter from her was just a terrible shock and the second letter was a great relief. The time in between was awful.

Sewing the front piece of Beach kept me busy. It was a joy, as I was making this with David. But most of the time I was alone,

I could feel my belly growing larger with each week. I'd see little poke- outs on my tummy when I was sitting--his foot as he stretched his leg, an elbow when he turned--this baby was telling me he needed more room. I would shift and the bump would go away but it would remind me that he--or she--was growing and was going to have to come out someday. I'd break out in a sweat when I remembered Mandy's birthings. She hadn't had any bad trouble, but I could see it wasn't a comfortable experience. Hadn't bothered me when it was her. It was different now that it was me.

When I made the backside of the quilt, I changed my mind about the solid gray. I pulled out the patterned materials I'd stuffed back into the bag. The old cloth with family memories gave me comfort. Everybody had troubles; most made it through. I made large squares of crazy quilt with the patterns and joined them together. When I closed up the whole thing I made a frame for both front and back from Zack's gray Army blankets. Later, I embroidered yellow suns around the edges.

I was pregnant, I was alone, I was afraid, and I despaired that David would ever be mine. The nights were long and so lonely.

But, like everything else, I lived through it. The change when it came took me by surprise, though why I can't say now, as I should have been expecting it.

David usually did get what he wanted.

15. TONIGHT, HE'S YOURS

The more bored and lonely I got, the more David insisted I come with him and Amy. I was strong willed, but, I tell you, Annie, to me nothing was worse than that continual fog and rain. If I'd been well, maybe I could have stood it, but I had heartburn, my legs cramped up at night, my back ached and I was so bloated I felt about to bust sometimes. Still I might of stuck it out 'til the baby was born if I hadn't fallen.

I was coming back from the woodshed, my arms full of wood for the fire so I could fix David's lunch. I slipped on the dang beach grass and landed flat on my rump. I didn't hurt myself, but David was just coming down from his place and saw me fall. He helped me up and made sure I was all right but didn't say anything about it. That should have been a warning, because David could carry on something fierce about the littlest problems I had.

That evening there was a light knock on the door. I thought David was being gentle because he didn't want to disturb me in case I was asleep.

When I opened the door a woman was standing there. I knew immediately she was Amy. She was not a timid woman. She stepped into the room. Right off I sensed the power and downright good sense of her. She was shorter than me, but not little. That night she had on a dark green cape that showed her eyes were more hazel than the brown Willie had described. She fixed them on me as she shut the door behind her. Standing just inside the door she undid the ties of her cape, still silent. The hood fell back. She shook her hair to lift the blond curls of her bangs where the hood had flattened them. I guess her hair had grown since Willie had seen her on the beach with David. She'd pulled it up into a soft bun from which some strands had escaped, falling down onto her shoulders. She was a pretty thing.

She took the cape off and laid it over the back of one of the kitchen chairs. Of all things, she was wearing a crème colored silk blouse that she'd tucked neatly into a tailored brown skirt. She was wearing pearls, for Pete's sake. Dressed to kill--only time I ever saw her dressed like that. Usually she wore her hair in braids and plain cotton clothes for working around the house. She was sensible though. Her shoes were sturdy black oxfords. She wouldn't have slipped coming down the path from their place.

I'd moved over back up against the table when she reached for me. I couldn't move.

"Dear Sophie," she said as she took my hand.

Dear?

She plunged to the point. "David tells me you fell today. Certainly you know you cannot be alone any longer. It's totally unnecessary." The small movements on my part to pull my hand from her grasp were ignored.

"David wants you with us..."

"Did he send you?" I was angry at this woman. And David. She was upsetting all my notions about her. I preferred to think of her, when I allowed myself to think of her at all, as a woman desperate for her husband's love. A woman willing to do as he bid her. A meek, submissive little nobody who secretly hated me but desperately kept it from David with her soups and sweet inquiries about my health.

"No. He didn't." She released my hand. "When I told him I was coming he tried to stop me, and then he wanted to come with me. But the talk we must have can't be done with him around. Now..."

She sat down, completely at ease. She motioned me to do the same.

That irritated me. It was, after all, my house. In defiance I chose to sit on the edge of my chair, to show I would do as I pleased in my own home, not as she bid me. I wanted her to know that I was not as malleable as she.

"I understand from David that you think his idea of us all living together is crazy, perhaps immoral. Gosh, I hope you're not right. As you know, David isn't like other men. That's why I love him so. If we're going to make this all turn out so that no one gets hurt--well, no more than can be helped--we're going to have to do something unusual. And we have the baby to think of."

I sat quiet, no words in me, as she explained what she wanted me, us, to do, and why. Punkin Sue Tiger lay curled up behind the door, among my boots and clamming gear, waiting for the stranger to go away. His eyes were fixed on Amy as she talked.

"For as long as I've known him, David has approached things with a different viewpoint from most people. He proposed to me when he was seven and I was only five. Even then I knew he was different. He watched everything everyone did and knew instinctively which things made people happy and what tormented them. He had a reverence for marriage and love that you probably find confusing, considering the circumstances you find yourself in. But David knows that the only way to hold a love is with open arms. There is the danger your mate will fly away, yes, but what's sadder than an animal caught in a trap? I've seen it in the eyes of too many people wedded for life to their one-and-only."

She almost made sense. I thought of my sister Mandy and her husband, of my mom and dad. I'd seen the look. But I'd never known what caused it. Maybe Amy and David were right. I never knew a happier married couple.

"Maybe it makes a little more sense to you now." She saw my hand trying to cover the big belly that seemed to me to fill the room. "That is not the point right now.

"If you don't move up with us, one of us will have to come down here and be with you." She was stating it as a fact, unquestioned. She wasn't asking if I agreed.

I could have argued. I could have refused, like I had with David, but what good would it have done? I'd still have had to see them every day--both of them--I was sure Amy wouldn't let me be alone now.

Before I gave in, I had a question that had been bothering me from David's first mention of me living with them. Her frankness made me bold. Okay, I might live with them, but... "Where-where would I...?"

Amy raised her eyebrows. "Where would you sleep?"

I felt my face flush. I looked over her shoulder, at the wall, at the dark window, at Punkin Sue Tiger peeking out from between my beach boots. Everywhere but at her, especially not at the clear gaze of her eyes. If I thought my stomach seemed big before, now it was gigantic, the only thing in the room.

She knew I was embarrassed, but she just shrugged her shoulders, and laughed, a little shakily. "Frankly that has bothered me, too. But I think that if we face it head on we'll be okay." Quickly, as if to get the pain over as fast as possible, like ripping off a cover over a sore, she told me I'd be sleeping in what had been the storage room. It was all ready for me with my own bed, and had been for weeks.

As for where David would sleep..."The only way to prevent problems between us, you and me, is to share him.

"You know." Again that quiet laugh. "This is the first time I've ever had to actually practice what David, and I preach. I hope you'll help me."

I was anxious to have her keep talking, I nodded.

She looked uncomfortable when she rose and stood at
the window, looking out into the now-dark night.

"David will spend one night with you, the next with me, and
then with you again." She took a deep breath. "And so on." She
turned toward me again. No tears. There was a sadness in her eyes
that had not been there before.

I suppose she'd dealt with her own devils long before tonight.
After a quick sigh the look was gone; I only saw it once again.

Oddly, it was that quick look of sadness that convinced me.
Up 'til then I'd feared that Amy, like David, saw no pitfalls in this
scheme. She knew as well as I the dangerous thing we were
attempting, but she was willing, for David's sake, and the baby's, to
give it all she had.

And I knew at that moment with an intuition rare to me, that
she would do whatever she needed to do to save her marriage.
That's when I put away the last small hope I had that I could
wiggle David away from her.

I was lighter, my belly felt normal, baby-sized again. It took
little effort to go to her, take her hands in mine and say, "Okay.
We'll do it." She knew I meant she and I, not David. She squeezed
my hands, sealing our bargain. I pulled my hands away, wanting
now to get this closeness over with.

While she waited and played with Punkin Sue Tiger, I
gathered up my nightclothes and a few toilet articles. I hesitated a
moment, then blew out the lamp and followed her out the door.
The path was dark, and slippery. This way was new to me. She
reached around, took my hand and led me. The surf pounded
below us, the only sound in an otherwise soundless night. The only
light in our dark world came from the house she was leading me to.

My mind was spinning. I realized we'd left Punkin Sue Tiger
and started to turn back to get him. She misunderstood

my move and tightened her grip. I didn't explain. He'd be all right tonight, I could get him in the morning.

The morning. The night. Right now, I didn't know which I feared more.

I concentrated on the sound of the waves landing on the sand to avoid thinking about what she was leading us to. My instinct was to turn and run.

Amy's hand tightened on mine. The light from the house grew brighter as we got closer.

Just as we got to the door Amy stopped. Through a fog of near-panic, I heard her say, "Tonight, he's yours."

She gave me no time to answer, her hand turned the doorknob. With her palm strong on my back, we entered her home, together.

Threads

PART TWO

16. NAMES ON A QUILT

Once Aunt Sophie started reliving the days of sixty years ago, it was as if her dammed up memory started flooding. She continued talking as we picked the rest of the berries, took them home, washed and picked them over.

From the basement I could hear her talking while I packed a few boxes with empty jars. Upstairs she interrupted her story only to direct me in scrubbing the dusty jars and sterilizing them in boiling water to make them ready for the bubbling jam. We put up fourteen jars and had enough left over to make three small pies for the freezer.

The kitchen was small and old-fashioned, like the house. It belonged to my Uncle Boyd, Mandy's fifth child, whom Aunt Sophie had declared would probably turn out to be undependable, a roving artist perhaps. He certainly would not be the one to support Granny Mandy in her old age.

He delighted Aunt Sophie by walking and talking early, and he became her favorite nephew. Because he was her favorite, and perhaps reminded her of her own child, she had given him more attention and was harder on him than any of the others. As he grew, and his talent for drawing and comedy became more and more pronounced, she encouraged and, some say, harassed him to apply himself to his talents and his studies. Through her influence he finished high school two years early. And then to her dismay, he left home, or fled, to wander about the country, picking up work where he could.

Boyd had a curiosity about people that, coupled with a fascination about how they governed their lives, led him to watching more closely the activities of those who are entrusted with power to govern for all: politicians. He sought jobs with small town newspapers. His knack for discovering who really ran what, and why, and reporting it clearly and humorously in succinct cartoons, led him to Washington, where he drew his cartoons for the most loved, or most hated, paper in the Capital.

Nationally famous, he turned homeward to the person responsible for developing his close observation of people, his discipline, and his unwavering honesty--Aunt Sophie. On one of his trips he decided to buy a parcel of Oregon ,"To come home to." He found the small house with a few apple trees, plum and peach trees, and edging the property, blackberries. There was also a Royal Ann cherry tree, and a pear. A small stream ran through the back. Aunt Sophie fell in love with the place, so Uncle Boyd asked if she would do him a favor, live in it and take care of it for him. There's no doubt in me that he planned it all along.

She lived there for close to twenty-five years. On the rough walls of the outhouse she pasted quotations by Thoreau, pictures cut from magazines--many of the sea--and poems she liked. Robert Service's "The Cremation of Sam Magee" was a favorite.

"The Cremation" covered much of the door. The relatives said such silliness just proved Sophie wasn't all there. But I loved it, even at night when I couldn't read it. It tickled me just to know it was there, to think of the line, "...I didn't like to hear him sizzle so."

When a picture or poem got too wrinkled and spotty from the dampness, she just pasted over it. The inside of the outhouse became a hodgepodge collage of art that appealed to her. Another thing that pleased me was that the outhouse was a two-holer, with one of the holes being child-sized. I never like those big holes with all the dark below.

86

In Aunt Sophie's last years Uncle Boyd added on to the little house, making room for an indoor bathroom. The outhouse collage was lost, but she wrote up a new copy of "The Cremation" and put it on the inside of her bathroom door. She had a sense of fun, Aunt Sophie did.

The house's two bedrooms were small, one upstairs reached by a narrow stairwell, one off the living room. The kitchen and pantry were miracles of planning. Shelves lined the walls and hooks hung from the ceiling, all in use. Dried herbs hung next to the wood stove she used for cooking and heating. The wood cook stove was there even after Uncle Boyd had the place electrically wired. That was when he had a small refrigerator put in. Sophie admitted the electric lights were better for the close needlework she did, and electric heat in the winter was convenient on cold nights, but she never gave up the morning warmth and comfort of a wood fire in the kitchen stove. There was also a small, stone fireplace in the living room. On wintery nights she would build a fire. She watched the flames or listened to the crackle of the fire while she, "...stitched something up." I believe that is the main reason she loved the house so; the fireplace reminded her of the one in David and Amy's house.

The fireplace, and the little bedroom upstairs. It was Uncle Boyd's room. There was a high, four-poster bed, and mirrored chest of drawers. His fishing gear and hunting and camping clothes hung on nails behind the door. A mounted deer's head stared at us from the wall--I guess it was his. It always kinda spooked us kids. Other than the deer head, the room looked more like a child's room than a man's.

A box in the closet held an elaborate electric train that we sometimes set up on the floor. A slingshot hung on a peg on the wall. There were toy trucks and cars on the windowsill. On rainy days we cousins pulled a puzzle box off a shelf and, depending on the intricacy of the design, amused ourselves for hours. Over the years our parents had filled the bookcase under the sloping roof with blocks and books, and sometimes we even took them out, read or played with them. But more often we mixed up the trucks and cars, the toy farms, the blocks and the boy and girl dolls, into stories we made up to amuse ourselves. It was essentially a boy's room, one where you did something, didn't just sit around reading or coloring.

Whenever us children stayed with Aunt Sophie, and we did as often as possible, the room was ours. There was a familiar warmth about it, not only because I spent so many nights playing and sleeping there, but because it was always the same.

My favorite thing in the room was the quilt on the four-poster. A simple tied quilt with bright colored squares, the design fascinated me, and the other cousins, for it was embroidered every which way with names. The whole family was there, all the aunts, uncles, cousins, and grandparents. I was up near the top so that my name was raised by the pillow when the bed was made up. We called it the Name Quilt.

When bored I'd read the names and take comfort in being surrounded by all the people I loved, and even some I didn't but who were nevertheless of my blood. There was a mystery contained in the quilt. The names in the center, below "Sophie Elm" did not belong to us: David Smithers, Amy Smithers, and, in bright blue, J. Sampson Smithers and Lily Smithers. None of the other names were in such a bright color. The first time the oddness of it struck me I was about eight or nine. I puzzled over the names, trying to fit them to some relative seldom heard of or some long dead ancestor. I finally took the mystery to my aunt to solve.

She was no help. "Oh, those are some people I used to know a long time ago who I was very fond of. They don't mean anything to you." That only made me more curious. After much nagging through the years I got no further than a promise that maybe some day she would tell me about them, but she'd always deflect penetrating questions.

"Just look at your hands." I curled them tightly into my brown palms. "Aren't you ashamed to have such dirty fingernails?" I was. One of the penalties of staying with Aunt Sophie was having to adhere to her standards of how neat a little girl should be. Clean and neatly rounded fingernails, clean and untangled hair, which meant tight braids, or, if I was lucky, or she had the time, ringlets.

And every night without fail, visiting children suffered a maddening tickling, lying flat on our backs in bed while she squeezed a dropper of chilly fluid into our noses.

"Stop squirming, and be quiet,' she would demand. "It's no skin off my back if you catch cold, but as long as you're with me you can at least try to help yourself." She swore the drops kept us from catching colds. I don't know what her medical information was but we tried not to sneeze or drip when we were with her. The only relief from this maternal torture was reaching the magic age of thirteen.

"Now you're thirteen, you should be able to take care of yourself," she stated, when, a few days after my birthday I lay, apprehensive, beside my ten-year-old cousin Teri as she suffered the drops. Finished with Teri, she handed me the bottle. "At least as far as drippy noses is concerned." She left the room. I knew I was supposed to put the dang drops in my own nose, but, grinning at Teri I just set the bottle on the bed table.

"More for you." I said.

Now I had forgotten the mystery of the names, but upon her first statement of, "David was mine," I remembered.

The blackberries were finally put up and stored on the pantry shelves. Aunt Sophie took a nap in her back bedroom and I went upstairs to rest on the four-poster bed. As always I checked my name first. Annie Elm. It was now quite worn as were most of the cousins' names, from our eternal running of our fingers over them. But David, Amy, J. Sampson and Lily Smithers were scarcely touched. I felt of them now, tracing the letters gently in some wonder, as if meeting new, but old, friends for the first time. The quilt held less mystery, but more warmth than ever.

J. Sampson was still an unknown, but he was definitely kin to me.
Aunt Sophie stopped talking only when we were done with the blackberries. The kitchen smelled sweet, the counters were sticky from berry juice and sugar, the room was hot and damp from our work and all the boiling of water and berries.

"We've earned a rest, my girl," she said, as she wiped her forehead with the bottom of her apron before taking it off. She sounded as tired as me. I was relieved to go upstairs and open the window to let the little breeze of the late afternoon into the room.

As I laid the thin quilt aside to nap on the sheets in the hot room, I didn't think of gray-haired Aunt Sophie downstairs, tired from a hard day's work, but of young, black-haired, perhaps even lusty--the thought was still difficult to admit--Sophie, as young as myself, and obviously not so innocent as I'd always thought.

After our naps, the evening cooled off enough that I brought in a few pieces of wood and stacked them by the fireplace. We ate tomato sandwiches with pieces of cheese and apple, drinking buttermilk in front of a small fire, 'cause she knew I liked it, not for need of warmth. After dinner she got out an afghan she was knitting, and with very little prodding, she picked up her story again.

17. THEIR ROOM, MY ROOM

The whole lower floor was one big living room. The large fireplace was the first thing I saw clearly, almost as clearly as I saw David coming toward me. Amy's hand dropped from my back; I was alone.

David's face at that moment is as clear to me now as if I had taken a photograph. His eyes were especially bright, his face was flushed from the fire, his hair was slightly dark and wet with comb marks. His usual grin was absent, his sweet mouth slightly open like he'd been breathing deeply. I must of looked as frightened as I felt, because his expression changed as he reached for me. His forehead wrinkled and his mouth tightened at the corners.

As aware as I was of David, I was even more aware of Amy, she was a blur of movement. While I stood frozen by the door and David moved in slow-motion towards me, Amy was busy to an extreme.

She'd thrown her coat onto a peg behind the door. I heard pans being banged around and dinner being made. Now faced with David, I wanted to flee to the safety of women's work with Amy, but stood rooted to the spot.

Almost without me being aware of it, David reached me and gently, hugged me. He would have kissed me right on the mouth, but I squirmed away so he only brushed my cheek. Amy was right in the same room. I tried to cover my embarrassment with movement, like Amy was doing. I struggled to get out of my coat, David helped me, then hung it up beside his and Amy's.

We stood still for a long time and even the kitchen area was quiet. I saw Amy looking at us, her face without expression. She caught my glance and once again she was full of purpose, her eyes focused on her husband. "David, take Sophie to the fire. She must be cold." It broke the spell.

"I was just going to. Sophie, you must be cold."

"Well, I'm just a little chilly," I admitted. In truth, a cold fear shook my very heart.

David put his arm easily around my shoulders and sat me in his chair by the fireplace, pulling up a stool for himself. He no sooner sat down than he was up again, poking at the fire, adding another small log from a hole in the right side of the fireplace.

"What a beautiful fireplace. I like this room." I chattered on about the room until David regained his composure.

He and Amy filled the evening with stories of how they'd found this area, selected the place, built the house, how happy they were with it but there were improvements they wanted to add. Amy made coffee and fried ham sandwiches, which we ate at a table set close to the big window facing the sea. The view was the same as mine but more so, including my cabin.

Every time either of them stopped talking, I asked another question about something in the room, a piece of furniture, the house plants, a pretty or interesting picture on the wall. I wanted to listen to them talk all night. The thought of what lay ahead petrified me.

After what seemed like hours, the talk ran out. We sat at the table in the stillness, with only a slight popping from the fire and an occasional hiss as a rain drop fell through the chimney into the flames. We could hear the ocean but the sounds within the room were most noticeable. I wanted to run out the door and down the path and into my cabin and lock the door.

Instead, I sat, waiting.

Amy breathed a deep sigh, which was loud in the quiet room.

"Well." She stood up. "Might as well do the dishes."

"I'll help." My voice sounded strange. I picked up my dish and lurched up to help her, relieved to end the stillness, to have something to do that would further prolong the, I now know, inevitable step. But that wasn't her intent.

"No." She took the plate from my hand. "David, take Sophie to her--" She corrected herself. "To your room. She's tired and needs to sleep."

Amy was right. At that moment I wanted nothing more than to be in bed, away from her, however normal she was trying to make this all seem. I wanted to escape. First most in my mind were her words just before we had come in, that David was mine.

Did she mean it? What was going to happen now?

Though it was David's idea and my final compliance that had got us into this situation, it was Amy who had managed this step to get me into the house. She'd helped smooth the evening with almost normal talk. David now needed to regain control, and so he did.

"Sophie, the staircase is right over there. The, uh, your room is to the right. I'll be up in a few minutes." I took my bag from beside the door and David led me to the steps which he didn't need to do as they were right in plain sight. I'd been aware of them all evening.

He said again, "I'll be right up." As I started up he called, "Be careful, the steps are steep."

I didn't need that advice, either. In my heavy and frightened condition all I could do was lug myself slowly and carefully up the steps. There were firm rails on either side, which helped some but two rails weren't necessary. Before I was ready, I was at the top. Their room was at the left, over the living room; my room was to the right, over the kitchen. So long as I lived there I never stopped thinking of them as their room and my room.

I no sooner got to my room and set my bag on the bed than I realized that I hadn't gone to the bathroom. It had been a nagging fullness all evening, I'd ignored it. I wasn't going to make it through the night. I looked under the bed. No chamber pot. Lord!

I wanted to stay in the room but I had to go. I left my bag on the floor by the bed and headed back for the stairs. I wasn't trying to be sneaky, I was concentrating on being careful as I came down the stairs. I got to the bottom with so little noise that they didn't notice me.

They were by the sink, with his arms around her in a loving embrace. She was kissing his face, murmuring, "I know. It's okay. I love you, too."

I felt sick. The jealousy I'd kept submerged all evening--along with my bladder ache--surged through me. I rushed through the room for the door.

"Sophie! What's--" I heard David call.

I mumbled something about the outhouse and was out before they could stop me. It was cold and raining which calmed the nausea I'd felt. I stumbled through the salal around the house, making noise that woke the chickens in the coop to the back of the house. Their squawking startled me until I could laugh and relax enough to search out the wooden walk running to the outhouse in the back.

While in there I considered heading down to my cabin and Punkin Sue Tiger. But I'd just have to go through all this again, unless I ran away. Where would I go? There was nothing to do but go back. I stopped by the coop and whispered to the chickens until I got my courage up to go back into the house. It felt odd opening the door, so I knocked lightly before going in.

Amy had finished the dishes and was sweeping up. The house was clean already; it was busy work. Now that the moment was at hand, she had nothing more to say. David was nowhere in sight. I went straight to the stairs, not having much to say myself. I forced myself to say, "Good night."

"'Nite," I thought she didn't appreciate me breaking up her last moment with David.

When I got to my room I found David already there. He'd lit the lantern on the bedside table and was already in bed. I pushed the door shut. He watched me undress and put on my nightgown and smiled as I tugged it over my big tummy. I'd made one 'specially big for my condition, but before long I had given it up and made a bigger one.

I was glad to blow out the light but shy about getting into bed with him. He pulled back the covers and moved over to make room. If I was an artist like David I could still draw that scene, my memory is so clear with it. Once I was in, he snuggled close. I finally relaxed and turned to him. We kissed for a long time, but didn't make love. I could never have relaxed enough for that on my first night in their house. It wouldn't have felt right.

I heard Amy come up the stairs and cross the hall into their room. I held my breath until I heard the door close.

He played with moving the baby around by pressing down easy on the little foot that poked up on my tummy, which made the baby shift inside me. We giggled and he did it again until I made him stop, I was afraid he might hurt the baby somehow even though his hands were so very gentle.

His love for me and the safety I felt in that bed, that first night and every night thereafter, completely overwhelmed me. I cried quiet tears and he comforted me, his hand stroking my skin in a way he never had before. Protective.

I felt safe with him. David went to sleep long before I did. I lay there feeling him close to me, listening to the night sounds of surf and the rain on the roof. I finally fell asleep.

18. LET ME SERVE YOU...

I woke in the near dawn to David smoothing the blanket over me. He was already out of bed, leaning down, when he saw my eyes open.

He kissed me and whispered, "I must fix the fire. Go back to sleep. Come down when you're ready."

I knew he was going to spend some time with Amy before I showed up downstairs, but, somehow, it didn't worry me.

The daylight of early morning woke me. My place in the bed was warm. I put my hand over to where David had been, it was cool. I could feel the chill of the room on my face. I snuggled the covers up close around my neck. I didn't want to get up. Besides, I was scared again.

Nature's call forced me to leave the room, or I might be there still. The morning was easier than the night had been. The coolness that Amy had showed the night before was gone. She was easy with me, no hint that we'd spent the night any different from usual.

She sat at the table with piles of paper spread in front of her. Her hair was loosed from the bun of the night before, now caught up into a soft braid tied with a brown ribbon. She smiled at me as I came from the stairs across to her, said, "Good morning, dear," and moved her hand to invite me to sit down at the table with her.

"Not yet." I smiled back at her, it was impossible not to. "I'll be right back." Grateful for a normal reason to not stop and chat, I went out into a beautiful morning. The ground wasn't dry but the sky was, for which I thanked the gods. I breathed in probably the first comfortable breath I'd taken in weeks, and took the side walk to the house out back.

After I'd taken care of nature I walked around the ground for a few minutes, looking at the bushes and stumpy trees, just getting comfortable with being there. The chickens were already out of the coop, David must have been here. Maybe Amy took care of the chickens? It was something I could help with. I peeked in to look for eggs. The nests were at the back, not enough light for me to see whether they held eggs or not. I'd have gone in but a rooster left the group of hens and flew at me, screeching and threatening. Whoa! I backed up, not ready to challenge him.

I'd not taken a wrap so when the frosty air began to sink in I gathered my courage and went back into the house.

"David's in the gable, painting," Amy said, indicating again a place at the table for me.

The room was warm from coals in the fireplace. I picked up a piece of wood from the box by the hearth and put it on the fire. Puttering around. "It's really cold this morning."

I know she could hear the fear in my voice. Less than the night before, but still there.

She rose from the table. "Are you hungry?" She went to the sideboard and pulled a loaf of bread from the box there, and began slicing.

"I am," I said, "a little."

"No wonder." She opened the oven door, putting the bread on the rack, and then put a couple of pieces of wood in the stove firebox. The smell of toast filled the room.

"There's oatmeal on the stove, and bowls up here." She indicated a shelf above and to the side of the stove before she went to the foot of the stairs. There was a narrow pull rope there that I hadn't noticed the night before. She pulled it, sounding a bell way above us.

"David. In the gable. I know he'll want to eat something, and see that you are okay."

I had the grace to blush.

She had the grace to pretend she didn't notice.

We could hear David coming down the stairs. She remarked on how pretty the frosty morning was and I said I thought so too. David was a relief, turning the corner at the bottom of the stairs and coming across the room to the kitchen table. He hesitated--this was new to him too--and then brushed his hand over my hair, a loving gesture that calmed me down.

He pulled out my chair. "Let me serve you, my lovelies." He filled three bowls with mush, put out spoons for us each, and sat down. Amy had already brought the toast to the table where I'd buttered it, thankful for the work. I pushed the toast plate to the center of the table while she sat down, handing us each a napkin.

I started to reach for my oatmeal.

"David," Amy said.

His head was already bowed. "Thank you, Lord. Amen." He lifted his head, smiled a big smile at both of us, and began spooning sugar on his oatmeal. We all three relaxed.

It was our first meal together, the first of many. We fell into a pattern that lasted for most of my time there: I prepared breakfast, for which I always set an attractive table, if I do say so myself. David fixed lunch and, while I took a late afternoon nap, Amy cooked dinner. The other chores got done easily. David helped where needed and sometimes when not needed.

Amy confided to me once when he was gone on his morning beach walk that he'd seldom helped around the house before, other than wood chopping and fixing things. The only reason we could come up with was that when we worked and he sat, there was too much suggestion of a harem serving their lord, and David certainly didn't want that. At least he said he didn't.

I loved the chicken coop that David had built. It looked more like a real house than the big one did, but was small. It became part of my mornings to collect the eggs. Walking among the chickens soothed me, listening to their soft cheeps and clucks as they pecked after bugs on the ground, or grabbed at the corn I threw out for them. After a few days the hens let me enter the coop without fuss and take their prizes. The rooster was crazy, never accepted me, but I flapped my arms back at him and screeched louder than him and he backed off enough for me to get into the coop. He would crow at odd hours of the night and couldn't be depended on as an alarm clock unless you wanted to get up in the middle of the night. By dawn he was often asleep, too tired from crowing through the night to greet the morning.

That first day went quickly. My initial impression of Amy was that she was a spotless housekeeper, because we cleaned all that first day. We washed down, straightened, and swept: cupboards, shelves, bedrooms, floors. She wouldn't allow me to do the heavy work so David asked me to take a walk on the beach with him. I thought Amy would like to have the house to herself for a while. We left.

He helped me down the slippery path. As we passed my cabin I heard Punkin Sue Tiger yowl from inside. I'd forgotten all about him. When I opened the door he ran out and raced around my feet, then around David's, crying loudly the whole time, both mad and glad I suppose. He ran off to the bushes.

"We can pick him up when we come back," David said, laughing.

I agreed with him. I was so in love with him that at that moment whatever he said, went. And I wanted to get down to the beach too.

Once there he put his arm around my waist and we walked close, our hips bumping. I began to feel my insides and bones softening, the first time since Amy's appearance at my door. The wind was bitterly cold, biting into my face and hands. David suggested we go back.

"Not just yet, please." I pulled him to a sheltered place below the cliff. In the privacy of a deserted beach I put my arms around him and hugged him close. Comforted, we sat on a damp log.

There, with winds that whipped away our voices beyond a couple of feet, I questioned him. "What does Amy think of your great plan now?"

For not the first time, and certainly not the last, David was exasperated with me. "I don't know why you continue to question her. Amy is as you see her. She has no secret dislike of you that she's hiding. She likes you. Of course..."

I knew it. He was about to admit that all was not rosy between them, her act was all a farce.

"She is worried about you working too hard, and wonders whether you'll miss having your family around when the baby comes. And she says you should have a doctor here when you deliver."

She was worried about me. Not about her and David. Of course she'd probably keep that to herself, but... My suspicion of her, most active when I was away from her, lessened.

David's hand was resting absentmindedly on my swollen belly. Suddenly the baby kicked and his hand flew off as if burnt. "Whoa! Who's in there? A tiger?"

He bent close to the mound. "Who are you in there? How's the weather, huh? Warmer than out here for sure. Be glad you've got such a nice nest. Soon you'll be out here playing on the beach with us. I'll show you how to build a sand castle and you can tell me what it was like in there. I've forgotten. What are you? That kick was a boy's kick. But maybe you're a strong girl like your mommy.

"Just wait till you meet your mommy. She's a funny lady, always asking questions when she should be quiet and being quiet when she should be asking questions."

He looked up at me and stroked the baby through my clothes. "Your mommy is beautiful, too." His eyes were tender and thoughtful.

I reached out and pulled him to me. I thought no more of Amy and what he'd said until a few days later.

But his mention of a tiger recalled me with a start, Punkin Sue Tiger, cold in the bushes. We left the chilly beach and rescued our unhappy cat. He settled into the new house like he'd always been there, part of the family.

That night I went to bed right after supper. The time after dinner was always easier for me on the nights he spent with her because it seemed, it was, more natural to me. I loved sleeping with him but never got used to it when she was in the next room.

19. THE ROOSTER CROWED AT DAWN

The days flowed one into another. After I'd been there for about two weeks Amy brought up the subject of a doctor.

I refused to consider it.

She pleaded, "If anything goes wrong I'll never forgive myself. Maybe if I'd had a doctor with my baby everything would have been all right." She saw the struck look on David's face. "But maybe not. We'd planned to, but I thought I had plenty of time. Some things just aren't meant to be, I guess. And look. We're going to have a baby anyway, even if it's not just as we thought it'd be."

I was embarrassed, but she didn't seem to be. That was her way. She accepted what was, not the way things were supposed to be. I'd always been at war with the facts, trying to turn things into something I can make sense of. I was used to things being natural and simple, and having a doctor didn't seem natural to me. They'd got me into their house, made me a part of their family so that I almost felt comfortable there, but on the subject of bringing in a stranger to help me in what I saw as a simple affair, I could not be budged. I was going to birth a child and wasn't married to the father, not even a doctor was going to know that. There would be no doctor.

During my last two months I was glad I wasn't alone. The

cabin had been so desperately lonely and now I was, in spite of myself, happy. David and Amy laughed a lot, talking and teasing each other with old stories of funny things that had happened to them. While we popped corn over the fire in the long-handled popper, we discussed the strange, unexplained, spooky things that raise the hairs on the back of your neck. On really stormy nights Amy would sit on the braided rug by the fireplace and play the flute. Sometimes David would sing softly and with very little coaxing I would join him.

In my eighth month, when the baby was seeming to be trying to kick his way out, we found that if Amy played soft and close to me the baby quieted down. He enjoyed the music too. The only one who wanted none of it was Punkin Sue Tiger. He'd either go sit by the door and meow to go out, or go up the stairs, and later I'd find him sleeping in the center of my bed. He was not a musical cat.

As my time neared I stayed around the house more. My heartburn was miserable and my stomach muscles started practicing for birth. It alarmed Amy and David more than me, because I'd seen it happen with Mandy's four births. It did spur me to a flurry of sewing and crocheting. Punkin Sue Tiger gave me fits with the thread.

David went into town and bought yards and yards of white flannel that Amy and I made into nightgowns and diapers. I embroidered the nightgowns with blue forget-me-nots and yellow daisies and we made a small flannel-backed quilt from my scrap bag.

David stopped painting for a while to finish a cradle. The wood was still there from when Amy was pregnant. He'd put it away when she lost the baby. Now he hummed to himself as he sanded and polished and carved. I sewed. While we worked Amy put away her sewing to play her music. It was all more natural than I could have believed.

Preparing for a baby should be the happiest thing humans do, and for us, it was. We were all excited but they were a little afraid, too. Neither of them had been around at the birth of a baby. David had been the youngest in his family and Amy's younger brother and sister had seemed to just be there with no notice.

I was afraid of the pain.

Mandy had carried on so with the births of her four that I determined not to scream if I could help it. I also knew that Mandy was more dramatic than me, and because she was angry at her husband for not being there, she made everyone, including herself, suffer. When he came home, after each birth, she gave him a blow by blow description of her suffering and swore never to go through it again. She wouldn't stop until he begged her to forgive him, and comforted her, promising never to be away again. But once she had the new baby in her arms she forgave and forgot and was happy the next time she was carrying another child.

My last week was the worst. March going out with a roar. The ocean stormed and the clouds poured the last heavy winter rains on us. On April third, the sea calmed down and the rain lessened to a drizzle. I felt more energetic than I had in days. I baked enough bread and rolls to last a week, then mopped the floor. I finally stopped, only because Amy was worried, and once she got me to stop I wanted to do nothing but rest. I went to bed early because she insisted. I wasn't physically tired, just wanted to be alone for a while. It was her night with David. I could hear their voices from downstairs, until her flute lulled me to sleep.

Early in the night I awoke. All was quiet, until I heard that crazy rooster crow. I figured that was what had wakened me, and tried to get comfortable again to go back to sleep.

A sharp tightening at the bottom of my belly brought me to attention. It felt different than the other cramps, deeper, more insistent. It passed and I lay waiting in the dark, alert. After an eternity it grabbed again. I kept quiet, not yet ready to share this with anyone. I was excited but protective of this miracle that was happening between my baby and me. I thought about the baby and prayed that all would go well.

The pains got harder, closer together and I didn't want to be alone any longer. I called out softly, "David." I no sooner said his name that he was in the room.

"Sophie? What's the matter? Is it the baby? Is it time?" His words tumbled in a rush of excitement and fear. He lit my lamp, took one look at me and shouted, "Amy!"

She must have been waiting for his call, she was there so quick. She took my hand as a contraction grabbed me, I squashed her hand in mine. She took charge.

"David, start the fire in our bedroom. Put clean sheets on the bed. We'll move her in there where it's warmer, and we'll need hot water to wash with."

While David hurried around getting everything ready, Amy sat with me, talking softly and holding my hand. When their room was ready she helped me from the bed. Warm water suddenly rolled down my legs. My bag of water had broken and I knew the birth was not far away.

Walking was difficult. It had been hard to get up. Now it was hard to get down into a bed again. David helped us into their room. Amy sent him downstairs to heat up more water and to scout out the old flannel sheets she'd put aside for this. She helped me into the bed.

"Well, Amy, this is it." I tried to joke between pains. "I hope you're ready. No more peace and quiet in this house."

She gave me her hands to pull on as a big wave of pain grabbed me. "I'm ready. We'll handle whatever comes. You just relax, and push."

Yes, indeed, relax. Easier said than done.

I didn't need any urging to push. My body was fixed on it.

She let go my hands and gave me a towel tied to the head of the bedstead to pull on. David came into the room.

His lips were tight around his mouth. He hovered over me.

"Are you okay? What can I do to help you? I'll rub your back." My back? He stepped back at my glare. "For God's sake, Soph, what should I do? Just tell me, I'll do it." He moved from one side of my bed to the other.

"Stop moving around. Give me your hand." When he did I shoved it away.

"You're hurting, I can tell. I don't know where to touch you."

"Don't touch me," I swept his hand off my forehead. "Lord, David. Can't you do anything ?"

"I'm trying."

I grunted, reached out to him. I wanted his hand. Despite myself I groaned. David grabbed my hand. I wasn't aware of anything other than trying to push the pain away. I wasn't thinking of the baby, just doing what my body demanded. When I got my breath I noticed how hot I was. David had built quite a fire. "David, please, open the window."

"It's cold out there."

"Well, it's hot in here. Please."

He opened the window a crack. That small coolness from the sea relaxed me until the next pain came. The next few minutes seemed to go on forever, until a final crushing squeeze in my back, belly and bottom. I felt the baby start to come out. One more push, it was over and the pain stopped.

David immediately shut the window.

Amy grabbed a flannel. With the stopping of the pain I focused on her. She scooped the baby up into the cloth as easy as if she'd always done it. His wail filled the room. My baby's face wasn't the only one wet. Tears streamed down Amy's face, and David's.

"For heavens' sake," I demanded, my own voice none too

steady, "Is it a boy, or a girl?"

"He's a little Sampson," Amy laughed through her tears. "A head full of hair and all." She handed him to David who put him on my flat belly. He brushed at his face with the back of his hand, and turned to help Amy. I paid no attention to the delivery of the afterbirth or the cutting of the cord I combed my baby's wet hair with my fingers. It was a black mass that went down to his neck.

We named him Jonathan Sampson but always called him Sampson, except when he was naughty, then he was Jonathan Sampson Smithers.

I had thought I was grown up and understood life, but it took Sampson's birth to show me the full range of it. As I lay there stroking his so soft, so perfect little body, I realized that he would die someday. I wanted to protect him from that and had to accept that, as I had not been able to prevent his birth, I could also not stop his death. But I swore I'd try to make his life pleasant and worthwhile, that I'd love him forever.

Light came through the window, along with the noise of the morning surf. That crazy rooster was just below the window and damned if he didn't crow at the dawn. For once he was on time and had something to crow about. He brought my thoughts back from death to life. We all grinned like we'd done something special.

The rain stopped and the early sun turned the room a rosy pink. Amy moved around cleaning up while David put some more wood on the fire. Sampson lay quietly beside me, looking up at me. His little face was so cute to watch. His forehead wrinkled and his mouth opened and shut. Such a tiny nose.

"Would you like some toast and egg?" Amy smoothed the blanket at the bottom of the bed, ready to leave the room. Her eyes glowed with a soft happiness. She was happy for me, and satisfied at the birth of our baby.

Little Sampson started at her voice, his head moving against my breast to find his breakfast, too. I loved that movement and never tired of it. "Yes," I said, "me too. This Sampson baby is gonna eat. We're starved."

She left the room to start the day's work.

David took his Bible from the top of the chest and sat down in the chair beside the bed. He looked at Sam and me, nodding as he opened the Bible to the front. Below,

Married:

Amy Johnston and David Smithers,

July 18, 1907

he wrote,

Born to:

Sophie Adele Elm and David Andrew Smithers:

Jonathan Sampson Smithers,

April 4, 1919.

May God bless.

20. LOVE OF WORK

Amy made me stay abed for a week. She wanted me to stay down at least two weeks but I wouldn't hear of it. I was restless to be up and about, sure that she was going to wear herself out running up and down the stairs, bringing my meals.

David was in the room with every little whimper from Sampson. I had plenty of milk and David delighted in watching me feed the baby. "Lucky boy, Sampson," he teased as the milk began to drip from my breasts whenever the baby cried to be fed.

He would lift Samson from his cradle, if he wasn't already holding him. Little Sampson's mouth would search for the milk, nuzzling into his chest. He'd lay Sampson beside me and watch with a grin as Sampson clamped greedily on a nipple and begin sucking with a fierce labor, his body softening as the milk flowed from my body to his.

I enjoyed it as much as they did, because my breasts were swollen with the milk and only Sampson could relieve it. We would both relax after he ate. David would burp him and put him back in my arms. Often I would waken, not knowing I had gone to sleep. David would be gone, and Sampson would be sleeping in his cradle, making his little snorty noises that were so sweet.

It was all very peaceful and enjoyable to rest and be waited on.

After one week I decided it was enough, time to get back to my own room and into our regular routine. They protested but I insisted, so we changed beds and bedrooms again. Sampson stayed in their room because it was warmer--we all said--and bigger. We all said, but we all really knew that as hungry as I was for this baby, Amy needed him. I wondered, later, of course, if that had been the best for me, but, that was later.

If Sampson woke at night to be fed, David brought him to me.

David slept for a week with me, mostly at Amy's urging, then we went back to every other night. Days, David took the cradle downstairs and we all gave Sampson so much attention that he seldom had a reason to cry.

Evenings I remember especially. He'd often whimper a little from gas or something; I'd lay him across my knees and rub his back and stroke his sides while Amy played her flute. It never failed to quiet him. His bright, big blue eyes would turn toward her and he'd kick his arms and legs and gurgle, almost as if he was trying to march and sing in time with the music.

When Sampson was so little, he could lay across my lap, then he grew enough to lay facing me lengthwise with my legs close together. I'd bring my knees up and play with his hands and tickle his belly. He especially liked the bee game. We'd all burst into giggles with him when I finished circling my finger with the funny buzz into his tummy or under his arm or under his chin.

David returned to his painting. He painted a picture of me nursing Sampson. He made me more beautiful than I was, with my hair falling loosely around my shoulders, and he caught Sampson's serious look of concentration, the furrowed forehead when he was working at dinner. He titled it "Love of Work." Although it was his best, he would not sell it. Most of his paintings that spring were a record of life within our house.

Amy returned to her writing and did a series of poems and short stories, some of them springing from the same well as David's drawings, Sampson. The poems concentrated on the wonder of birth, but the stories were tales of a small boy named

Sampson, and his adventures at his seaside home. They were wild fantasies of him taming sea lions and a whale, and riding over the waves on the backs of seagulls that came whenever he called. He had only to play his flute and all sorts of creatures came to play with him, a miniature Tarzan of the sea.

In late July, when Sampson was almost three months old, Amy began reluctantly to pack David's paintings and her writing for her annual trip to the city. She didn't want to go and worried that she was leaving us with no one to care for us. We just laughed and reassured her that we would be okay and told her to enjoy her vacation.

"Vacation?" She sputtered. "You two better hope I bring home plenty of money from my 'vacation'." She finally left, but planned to be gone for only a month. Even that was more than she could bear, she said, but what must be done, must be done.

I was surprised at how much I missed her in the house. We'd grown close and I loved her, but still I was looking forward to having David and the baby all to myself for a month. But the house seemed almost empty without her laughter and singing as we worked together or played with Sampson. He missed her too, and when we sat by the fire at night he would look bewildered when he whimpered and there was no Amy to play for him.

I think David missed her least of all, because he was used to her yearly absence and for once he had other people to talk to. It was now clear why he'd been so happy to have me when Amy was gone before. David hated being alone. The only difference that we both enjoyed from her departure was that we made love almost every night, but in my bed, not theirs.

She came back in early August, radiant. She burst into the house with David close behind, staggering under the load of her luggage. She'd gone with one trunk and the paintings and had come back minus the paintings but with two trunks.

Her brown eyes were dancing when she flew across the room and threw her arms around me. Her hug almost squeezed the breath out of me.

"I sold all of David's work the first week." She bubbled with happiness, lifting Sampson off the rug where he was laughing and trying to talk to her. "You little love!" She kissed him and held him out to admire him and pulled him close for another big hug. "You've grown so much. Auntie Amy missed you so much."

Another squeeze, he squealed, she calmed down and told us, "I spent the second week with a publisher. 'The Mother's Journal' bought all my poems and Springtime Books offered me a contract to publish all my Sampson stories in individual books, the first to come out next winter."

To say we were all happy to be together again and to have such good fortune to celebrate is to understate it. David killed a fat hen. We had chicken and dumplings, his favorite, in celebration, along with fresh lettuce and tomatoes from our garden, and blackberry pie for dessert. The new trunk sat by the door where David had dropped it when he'd dragged it in. It was heavy.

The house was a home again as we sat together at the table over coffee. Sampson was asleep in his almost too-small cradle by the fireplace. Amy was still bubbling and I wondered why. David and I were happy to have her back but we were puzzled at how she continued to laugh.

Finally, as the late summer sun began to set, she burst out with, "Well, you two. I have still another surprise. Bigger news even than the books and paintings."

She jumped up from the table and went to the new trunk. She fiddled with the catch, got it open and reached in. She had presents for us all. For me, a lovely dress of a deep rose color, and a beautiful pearl necklace. She helped me get the clasp fastened. I loved the feel of the pearls on my throat.

For David there were new pants, a shirt, a gold watch chain, and a cunning pocket watch that chimed off the hours. He wound it and then was immediately impatient for the hour to pass.

For Sampson a toy train that David wound up and watched it

run in circles on a small track. A small stuffed whale, that the baby grabbed onto, tasted, and held the softness against his cheek. Clothes enough to last until he was a bigger boy.

For herself, Amy had a rich, dark blue wool coat with a hat to match. She shrugged into the coat, set the hat on at a sassy angle and paraded around the room while we admired her. A light blue dress in the latest fashion, but no prettier than mine. And yards and yards of material. Satins, velvets, woolens, and lots of flannel.

"What's with all the flannel?" David said.

She threw her arms around him and then quieted down so I barely heard her say, "That's for nightgowns and bedding for our baby."

"Sampson has all he needs."

She put her fingers against his lips to shush him. "The new baby. Our baby."

After all the years of waiting, David's cup of babies was overflowing.

"Oh, Amy," was all he could say.

I got up and kissed them each on their foreheads and went to bed.

I lay sleepless, listening to smothered giggling and finally the soft notes of Amy's flute drifting upstairs. What would this mean to me, and to Sampson? Would Sampson be shoved aside? Would they love their baby more than him? I couldn't imagine it but I knew the power of blood enough to worry.

The next morning I learned that the last two weeks had been spent shopping, visiting friends, and seeing a doctor. She'd suspected she was pregnant when she left but had said nothing, for fear of another disappointment. It had really been the only reason she had gone, otherwise she would have sent David this time because she hadn't wanted to miss a whole month of Sampson's

growing. And, she said, she had missed me too.
"I'll never leave here again for that long." she declared, her
jaw as set as the night she had led me up the hill. "From now on
I'm a mother, and a writer, and David can be the salesman. Or get
the buyers to come here."

She was full of plans. "When the children are older we can all
take the train to Utah and show them off to Grandmas and
Grandpas and aunts and uncles galore."

"What did the doctor say?" I said.

"That I'm perfectly healthy, and as long as I'm careful I should
have no trouble. And you can bet I will be. Just to be sure though,
I'm going to see a doctor here. He advised it. And David wants me
to."

She was in her third month already, which relieved some of
our fear. Amy complained that we were treating her too delicately,
watching her like a pot about to boil over. We tried to treat her
condition as they had mine, with naturalness and joy, but there was
no getting around our worry over every little pain, and stepping in
to ease her way as we could. Despite her protests, Amy too took
care, moving slower and taking no chances. She would let
Sampson onto her lap but she didn't lift him there. She let him
crawl up, offering her hands for him to pull on. Once there he
snuggled easily into her. When he got restless she asked David or
me to lift him off. But truly she didn't have to take too much care
with that little baby boy. He sensed that she needed gentleness;
around her he moved more slowly. His heart and senses were like
his father, alert to his women.

We all eased Auntie Amy's way as much as we could. For
them it was a gentle winter and spring. For me, it was different.

21. A HOLLOW HOUSE

Sampson was crawling at six months. He had to be watched by someone all the time. If he was on his blanket on the floor he would crawl off to follow Daddy. We learned to watch him. Daddy decided that if he wanted to go so much, it was time for an adventure. On a fall day that was warm and with only a bare breeze, we packed a basket and took him for his first picnic at the beach.

I hadn't allowed David to take him before. I was afraid he would get sunburned, or catch cold, or some terrible thing. Getting down to the beach by the path, with the baby and our lunch basket, blanket, and a pregnant woman to maneuver, was a tricky job. The path was not slippery, but steep and with the slickness of dry sand.

It had never been a problem for my brothers or for David and me. It was a simple walkway from our cabins to the edge of the grass. There it became a sharp drop-off of about five feet cut into the sides of the bank, sloping to the sand. Through years of use it had rough steps easing the drop but the steps were ragged from a recent storm. The sides were close enough to grab onto beach grass if you started to slip.

I went first, with the basket. At the bottom David handed Sampson down to me.

"Don't start yet," he commanded Amy when she started down. He stepped directly in front of her, "Hold on to my shoulders." He led her down. At the bottom he stepped away, took Sampson from me and took the lead. Amy walked between us while I followed up with the lunch. Sure was easier when we didn't have to go through all this fuss.

We went to a secluded place David and I knew about. The grass was squashed flat. If Amy suspected why the area was so beat down she didn't mention it.

While David built a small fire to heat water for tea to go with our sandwiches, Amy and I spread a blanket on the sand. I laid Sampson on it. He immediately flipped over to all fours and started scooting forward. Straight to the sand, and a mouthful. I cleaned him up while Amy laughed. My cleaning annoyed David.

"A little sand isn't going to hurt him. Let him enjoy himself. He'll stop when it doesn't taste good anymore." I pulled Sampson back to the center of the blanket. I was rough when I brushed the sand from his mouth and hands. "Dirty boy! Shame!"

Both David and Amy were shocked. For the second time, I saw David begin to be angry. The baby started to cry. David pulled him away from me. He soothed him, "It's okay. The sand is nice, isn't it?"

He soon had Sampson laughing again but the first crack was there.

The picnic didn't go well. David knocked Amy's cup of tea over onto the blanket. Our argument had made her nervous and she lashed out at him, "Don't be so clumsy, David. You're worse than the baby."

He didn't answer, but got up and walked down the beach. In strained silence we watched him go over to Haystack Rock. The tide was far out that day so that most of the base was exposed. He poked around in the tide pools for about a half hour before he returned. He looked refreshed but his eyes were still a dark blue, a sure sign that he was still upset. Food would perhaps restore his spirits. Amy and I stumbled over each other's words in our eagerness to soothe him.

"There's still a bacon sandwich," Amy offered, while I held out a boiled egg. "I'll peel it if you like?" He shook his head, catching his upper lip with his bottom teeth, a mannerism he had that annoyed me.

"Nah, I've had all I need." He reached over to Sampson and chucked him under his chin. Sampson wiggled over towards him. "Hey, boy, I think the wind is coming up. What do you think?"

Sampson grinned at him.

Looking at Amy, David said, "We better go back to the house."

It was one of the few times that I felt left out, different, odd somehow. I didn't like it. I kept my fear inside me and didn't respond. I knew that Amy didn't want to go back, I could tell by the dismayed look on her face. She didn't come to the beach much since she had gotten bigger in the tummy. Sampson was having such a good time we all knew he was happy where he was. It was a beautiful day. But to argue with that set jaw would have been useless.

We packed the picnic gear back in the basket. Amy and I shook the blanket together. After folding it she hugged it close to her chest. David carried the basket, I carried Sampson, and Amy followed using the blanket as ballast.

She made a joke about it being easier back up the path since we were carrying the food inside us. I couldn't help grinning when David joked, "Yes, but you have a heavier load than we do," and patted her tummy.

David went up the path first. After setting the basket on the grass, he reached down and took Sampson from me. When I reached the top I took Sampson.

David turned to go back down to help Amy, but she was

already halfway up. He sucked in his breath. "Amy!" came out sharply.

She looked up, reached out a hand. The motion threw her off balance and she slipped, sliding back down the path. From his reaction you would have thought she'd fallen from a thirty-foot cliff rather than just slipping a few feet into loose sand. They fussed over each other at the bottom of the path. I stood there holding a squirming Sampson. I was as concerned as they were but I couldn't do anything. I knew she couldn't be hurt by that little fall but I didn't know about her baby.

I called, "Is Amy okay? Can I help?"

David mumbled something sounding like, "...don't know," and paid no more attention to me.

Finally, feeling forgotten and tired of trying to hold Sampson, I called down, "I'm going on up. I've got to put the baby down. I'll be back."

He looked up long enough for me to see the worry in his eyes. "No. That's okay. We'll be there soon."

The house sounded hollow, more so because I knew that David and Amy, though only a little ways away, were not with me at all. This pregnancy was their problem. That was evident whenever any problems arose. I could feel the weight of their years together before Sampson and I, came into their lives. Although we celebrated good times together and had shared my worries, this worry was not mine. I was only at the edge.

I busied myself washing up Sampson. He was cranky and tired and I was angry and didn't know why. With water that wasn't very warm, I scrubbed his naked little body, then went after the sand in his ears. He was as mad as I now. Scooping handfuls of water I splashed it into his ears and kept a firm hold around his slippery, fat little middle. He twisted away, got a face full of water, and let out a scream of pure mad. I yanked him from the basin and slapped him on his bare bottom. The CRACK was loud in what I thought was an empty room.

For a long second there was a silence after the noise, then the room filled with a deep, angry, "Sophie!" and a shocked, "Oh!" Sampson's howl poured over David and Amy's words.

Honestly, I was as horrified as they. I loved that little one more than my own life even, yet in a fit of despair I'd lashed out even quicker than I would have at one of Mandy's children. As bad as it was, and as I felt, I also was embarrassed that they had seen me spank the baby. I hadn't hurt him, but he screamed as if I'd tried to throttle him.

Amy rushed over. "Here, just let me take him."

I refused. I wrapped a towel around him and carried him past a white-lipped David to my bed upstairs where we both crawled under the covers and cried together. No one came up and soon the baby fell asleep. I was too ashamed to go downstairs. The heat of the day had made me sweaty, I was exhausted. Soon I slept too, Sampson's breath warm on my face.

It was almost dark when his soft pawing at my chest woke me. I gave him my breast, he latched on. The slurp was a peaceful happy sound and our sleep had erased our mutual anger. Full, he was easy to dress. His skin was cool from a breeze that came through the half-open window. I put him in a short cotton dress that left his legs free to crawl but covered his arms. The light blue lace at the neck and arms brought out the bright blue of his eyes, David's eyes. His face was pink with the sunset that shadowed the room. A surge of love for him and remorse for both of us swept through me, and I hugged him close.

His softness always amazed me. My happy boy giggled and his little hands grabbed onto my hair and tugged. I pried his fingers open and finally had my head free. He laughed and reached again for my hair, but I was too quick for him.

"No, no, naughty little Sampson," I cooed while I nibbled at his chubby fingers. He shrieked with joy, so I dropped him to the bed and attacked his cool toes.

"This little piggy went to market, this little piggy stayed home." I wiggled the sturdy middle toe. "This little piggy had roast beef, and this little piggy had none." By the time I reached, "...piggy cried all the way home," he was almost convulsed with laughter and waving his feet so that the last little piggy-toe slipped from my grasp.

I finished with kisses all over and bubbled my lips against his throat. He grabbed me around the neck and came up, clinging to me. I wrapped one arm around him and with my free hand grabbed a shawl from the top of the dresser and folded it around his back and chilly feet. We were ready to go downstairs.

I knew what we looked like when we came into the living room, compared to the way we'd left. My hair was mussed in a way that I knew David liked. Both Sampson and I were pink from our play.

The room smelled good, and safe. David was standing at the stove stirring a pot of beans. Amy, at the fireplace, put a log on the fire and politely nodded at us, then sat again in the padded rocker. The room with the small fire and warm food smell was very comfortable but the air was heavy with disapproval.

I felt I couldn't bear it if either of them mentioned the afternoon. The happiness I'd come downstairs with slipped away.

Cold fear from the pit of my stomach surged through me. I determined to pretend nothing had happened. I blew again on Sampson's neck and he giggled, which caused Amy to put down the book she'd picked up, and look at us, or rather, at Sampson.

She spoke directly to Sampson. "Oh, all happy now, huh?"

He babbled at her and, forcing a laugh, I handed him to her. "He wants his Auntie Amy." I talked to her through Sampson. "How are you, Aunt Amy?"

"Aunt Amy's just fine now." She took on the pretense, "Just a little tired."

"Well, then," I said brightly, "Mommy better help Daddy with dinner then," and turned before she could continue.

I crossed the room and, quickly and lightly, playfully, put my arm around David's shoulders and looked down into the pot. He didn't pull away from my touch but didn't lean in to me, either. My arm felt heavy.

"Beans, huh." My voice was forced but my fear drove me on. He was close, but distant. "Almost done?" I asked, softer, but it seemed that my voice cracked in an empty room. "Looks like you used up the last of the pork."

He mumbled, "Um huh."

I ignored the briefness of his answer and acted as if we'd had a normal conversation, and a normal day. "Well, I guess I got here just in time. How would you like some biscuits?"

A short, "Okay," from the man I loved and who now was avoiding looking at me as much as I was avoiding looking at him.

"And a little salad?" I still had my arm on his shoulder.

"I'll go," he said, still distant but I saw and felt his body relax a little, and the fear in my stomach loosened. He took the bucket from a nail on the wall by the door and left for the garden.

Making the quick biscuits gave me an armor against any but the lightest talk with Amy. That room that usually felt so spacious to me was now cramped, small. I mixed and rolled and cut while chatting on about new clothes for Sampson. Amy fell in with it, no more eager than I to renew the unpleasantness of the afternoon.

David came back with not only lettuce and tomatoes from the garden but new corn, a rare thing as the coast climate made it hard to grow. He was happier, lighter than when he'd left, perhaps because it was such a beautiful evening outside.

He put the corn on the table. It was already shucked, explaining why he'd been gone so long. I admired the small yellow ears while he put on a pan of water to boil.

The thing I feared most was silence so I talked and talked, about the corn, the garden, the lovely night, the baby, until finally they were drawn into the happy atmosphere I was working so hard to create. By the time we sat down to the table for dinner, with only the lamp and the fire for light, the coldness in my stomach had eased. Amy ate with Sampson on her lap, feeding him a bit of mashed bean now and then to keep his hands out of her plate. David finally gave him a scraped-clean carrot to hold and nibble on.

"Sophie and I are going to make Sampson some new clothes," Amy said.

"New clothes?" David smiled, and my spirits soared at the sight. "He already has more clothes than I do."

"Those are baby clothes. He's getting to be a little boy."

We were in such a hurry for him to grow up.

"His knees are red from crawling and I think a pair of pants would suit him just fine," Amy said.

"Pants?" David pretended to be shocked. "Why, I didn't wear long pants 'til I went to school."

"David, this is 1919, not the 1880's."

He started to protest but Amy cut him short. "We're going to cover his knees and that's that."

"Well," he said firmly, trying to maintain his control of things, ignoring our grins, "A big boy with long pants shouldn't be sitting on laps at the table." He reached over and tickled Sampson on his belly. "I'll start on your high chair tomorrow. How about that?"

Sampson arched his back and the carrot flew across the room. David got it, washed it, and handed it back. He promptly dropped it again. Sampson's game went on until David took him on his lap and held him until dinner was over.

The evening was quiet with Amy reading, me cleaning up and then sewing, and David trying to figure what he needed for the chair. Sampson lay rolling around his feet, playing with a stuffed doll.

We went to bed early with me deciding to have the baby in with me. I was glad it wasn't my night with David. I opened the window that looked out upon the ocean. The air was glorious and warm, reminding me almost painfully of the night on the beach that now seemed so long ago, when being here was all new, and I'd not yet met David. I wanted time before we slept together again. I wanted to snuggle close and if he'd pulled away, it would have scared me. Still, as always, I missed him and was grateful for the quiet snoring sound from Sampson's cradle close to my bed.

22. MERRY CHRISTMAS

*L*ife seemed to be again as it had been before the bad day but I noticed a strain in our easy- close feeling towards each other. I grew sharper with the baby as he started getting into things and it became more of a chore to keep him clean and unhurt. At seven months, Sampson was walking around the furniture, pulling himself up on the bookcase and pulling things down. By early December, going into his eighth month, we had to watch him all the time to keep him from crawling upstairs, or if someone went outside, he would scoot for the open door.

I started to feel like I had to do everything. Amy was approaching her seventh month, and, by the doctor's orders, she rested a lot, downstairs. She watched Sampson and played with him when she wasn't sewing, or reading, or writing. The main job, of course, of taking care of him was mine. David spent hours painting in their room because the coop was too cold. If the weather was even halfway decent I went out, taking Sampson, or, braving the cold wind, with David.

We'd pass my old cabin, with me feeling sorry for it being empty. I worried about the flowers. The rose bushes stayed hardy through the winter but they suffered as the wind sculpted them to parallel the house.

Whether with David, or with him and Sampson, when we got

down to the sand I was always cheered. I loved the briny smell of the ocean and the noisy waves, but I only needed a little bit of it. I worried about Sampson getting cold, or I'd start to think about making the bread to go with the soup we most always had simmering. I'd want the warmth of the house and back we'd go.

When Sampson wasn't with us, David and I once in a while stopped at my old cabin on the way back, to build a fire to warm the cabin and stave off the coast mold. "Just keeping it up for Mrs. Hawley." There I'd let David have his way with me--or I'd have mine with him--as the cabin warmed and dried. I loved being alone there with him, but as Amy's time grew closer so did our concern about leaving her for too long.

David enjoyed the winter, his first with two women and a small child to keep him company. I felt better than I had the previous winter, naturally, but there were more and more days of fog and rain which made me feel closed in. The last winter I'd hated because I'd been so terribly lonely and afraid. This winter was much easier, but still, by Christmas I was restless and we still had at least two more months of coast winter, and Amy's birthing to get through.

For Christmas David killed another hen, and I braved the cold to walk to the store in town to buy a small ham and apples. I made applesauce with cinnamon. David dug the last of our garden carrots. Amy boiled them and added butter and brown sugar. I made a rice pudding that Sampson loved--all over his face. We celebrated, as David said, "In style." Our gifts were few. I remember that Christmas so well.

It started early, with all of us up as soon as dawn broke. Amy and I were ready to open the presents that lay under the small tree David had cut from the woods behind the house. David wanted to eat breakfast first. Amy and I agreed that we could until we'd made coffee, but otherwise, why wait? Sampson was up, feeling our excitement, babbling and laughing. Amy looked at me in pretend despair. It was barely dawn. She flung her arms like she was giving up.

"If I live through a hundred and fifty Christmases with you,

David Smithers, God forbid, I'll never understand--" She turned
back to me, her eyes wide and eyebrows lifted. "I do understand
Sophie, I really do. He loves surprises, and he hates them." She
paused.

I said, "Explain it to me then. Is it something to do with a
man's stomach always coming first?"

David was pacing from the tree to the window looking over
the ocean, and back to the tree. "Here now, you two. Don't gang up
on me. I just think a little something, maybe a little oatmeal to tide
us over. You know we always--" He started toward the stove.

Amy blocked his way, her belly making a good barrier. "Yes, I
know 'we always' but this time we don't. This time we open our
presents first."

"But, why?"

"Because I say so, and you know better than to annoy a
pregnant woman." She gave him a little shove that tumbled him
into a chair.

"You see, Sophie," she said, as if David wasn't there, "he hates
it when it's all over. He waits so long. Christmas is his favorite
day. He fumbles around the packages, feeling this one and that,
doesn't matter if it's his or not. You saw him."

I had. Just like a kid, down on his knees prowling around the
tree, squeezing the presents.

Sampson didn't know the rules. All he knew was pretty colors
under, of all things, a big bush thing in the house. We all heard a
ri-i-p and, "Da Da," and saw Sampson waving a harmonica. As
with everything, it went straight to his mouth for a chew. One good
suck in the right place and he stopped in astonishment.

"What a smart boy." Amy handed him a present of his own.
"Would you like to start now?" She gave her gift of the harmonica
to David. "Or wait 'til your son does it all for you?"

"Seems I've got no choice. All three of you, I bet all four of you, are set on having things your way." Still, he waited until we were almost through with opening our presents before he started on his.

It wasn't just what we gave to each other that I remember so well from that Christmas, it was the absence of tension. No one was worried, or testy. Amy didn't worry about her baby. I didn't feel closed in or annoyed with Sampson, or feel left out when they talked about their baby. David relaxed because we did, and spent the whole day with us, instead of escaping to his paints. Sampson responded to the happiness and toys and pretty paper to throw around. David played checkers with me, and lost, but regained his manly superiority, as he called it, when he beat Amy at chess. The chess set was his gift to her. She teased him into another game and they were still at it when Sampson and I went to bed. Much, much later he woke me when he slid in beside me.

"Sorry," he whispered, "Didn't mean to wake you."

"It's okay," I whispered close to his ear. On impulse I nipped it sharply.

"Oho, woman! Think you can get away with that do you?" He tweaked my nose.

I grabbed his hand away.

He made quick little bites at my throat.

I was weak from keeping my giggling quiet and his hands to himself. Wanting him flushed through me so that I didn't, couldn't, didn't want to stop him. Sometimes I think of David, and that...fulfillment...that only...sexual love can know...

That night too, is why I cherish that Christmas memory so. It was the only time we made love with Amy there in the house. Maybe if I'd been more unbending about that...

23. YOU AREN'T AMY!

*A*unt Sophie seemed confused. We were both embarrassed. The fire was about out and it was late.

I suggested we go to bed. Quietly, we did.

After breakfast next morning, I eased her back into her memories as we worked on a couple of casual pants-suits I'd wear at work. My job is in a camera shop. I serve customers by day and have the use of the developing and printing equipment at night. It's an ideal setup because I can do my own printing of the shots I take on weekends and for special occasions of goings-on in town. The best ones I sell to our local newspaper. So far, the profits are small but I've reached the point where I receive more calls than I make, and that's encouraging.

I was anxious for Aunt Sophie to get her story finished. I wanted to know about what happened to Sampson? I feared the worst. It seemed more gentle, and easier, to start with the second baby.

"Did Amy have her baby all right?" I said, as we spread the cloth on the dining table and began pinning the pattern in place.

"Oh, Amy's baby." She paused, distracted, and straightened up from the table, a pin held in mid-air. In her eyes was a question as she turned to me.

"Didn't I... No, I guess I didn't. Well..." She bent again to the pattern and pushed the pin into the paper, joining it to the cloth, and picked up her story.

* * * *

The baby was due in early February. The doctor was going to come to the house when Amy started labor. That was the plan, but she came back from a visit to him in mid-January, upset.

It was raining, as usual. She came in with water dripping from her hat and coat. She pulled her hat off and threw it onto the shelf above the coat rack. Sampson babbled to her from the couch where he'd just pulled himself up. I helped her out of the wet coat and hung it over a chair to dry.

David sat her on another chair before the warming fire and undid her blond hair so it fell to just below her shoulder blades. She moved her neck around as he lifted and separated the wet strands. He took the brush from where he kept it on the mantle above the fireplace and teased out the damp clumps at her forehead down to the ends of her hair. Taking the comb that always lay beside the brush he straightened her drying hair, separated it into three strands which he plaited into a single braid down her back. His hands were gentle and sure, they had done this task many times. Amy's breathing slowed as she relaxed with his touch. It always soothed her when he put his hands in her hair.

She turned to look at me. "The doctor is leaving." She spoke in a rush, the words falling on top of each other.

"Sophie, he's going back to Portland. His father is old and not well, and he says there's not enough of a practice for him here since the road work slowed down. There's not enough people here."

David stroked her shoulders to calm her.

I didn't see that there was much of a problem. After all, I delivered without a doctor and so did my mother.

"I'll bet," I said to her, "that your mother didn't have one either."

"No, but with my brother and sister, David's mother was there."

I was hurt. "Amy, you know I'll be here. I've delivered all of Mandy's kids and they're all okay."

"Oh, I know, Sophie." Her forehead wrinkled and she screwed up her mouth. She was trying to be calm but couldn't hide her worry. She was scared. "I do trust you. You know I love you, but I wish... Oh! I wish my mother was here."

"She's not here. Mine wasn't either, you will remember. Looks like all you've got is me."

I was sorry for her distress at this unexpected turn but surprised that she was making such a fuss about it. I tried to soften my exasperation by adding, "And David. We've all been through this before. You'll see. It'll be all right."

David hadn't said much 'til now. His hands stopped moving, resting lightly on her back. "You're not going to have the baby here."

We both turned to look at him.

"Doctor James said there's a good doctor in Seaside and that's where you're going."

"Seaside?" we said together. "That's over eight miles away."

"It's closer than Portland. If a doctor can't come here, you will go to him." He struck the back of Sophie's chair with his fist.

She pulled away from his reach, looking at him, eyes wide, startled.

"Some doctor. All the time promising to be here, and then, just when you need him, leaving you alone."

I said, "But she won't be alone. I wasn't alone. I'll be here, like you were with me."

"You aren't Amy!"

I barely heard Amy's quick breath. "David."

For a second he looked confused, then his voice fell as he reached out to me.

"I only meant..." His eyes were wet with the hurt we both felt and, I'm sure now, with the fear he felt for Amy. "Sophie. You were, are, strong, and..."He fumbled for words. "Oh, Sophie, If anything happened...to Amy...to the baby...." His voice was low, serious.

You've got Sampson, I thought, unfairly, and guiltily, knowing I could never say it. I turned my head away. The thought had just popped in. I tried to keep my hot face hidden.

He put his hands on my shoulders and turned me toward him. "I'm sorry. I wouldn't hurt you for the world, Sophie." His eyes were sad. "I love you. But this is different."

My first flash of jealousy at Amy's baby was gone. I knew I was being foolish, though I didn't know why, yet.

"David." I straightened up. His hands fell from my shoulders but I reached up to his face, and touched his cheek lightly. "You're right." I looked at Amy. "I'm the one who is wrong. Of course I want what's best for Amy." Their strained faces relaxed a little. "And for your baby."

Briskly, I gathered my no-nonsense voice, not unlike the one Amy used on me when she came to my cabin. "And if it's a doctor in Seaside, I better get you ready."

Relieved, David said, almost cheerfully, "We all have to get ready. Four weeks for four people--five people." He stopped for a moment and pulled his shoulders back, as if adjusting a new weight. "In Resort City. We have lots of work to do."

He could be so annoying. "David, you obviously haven't thought this out. How do you know it's going to be four weeks?"

"Two weeks 'til the baby comes and two weeks after for Amy and the baby to rest." He was smug about his mathematics.

Amy and I looked at him. She spoke up first. "It might be longer, it might be sooner. Babies don't always follow the schedules we set up."

I said, "You can't know for sure how long you'll be gone, and Sampson would drive us crazy cooped up in a strange place. It'll be easier on all of us and less expensive if he and I stay." I looked at Amy. "Although I wanted to be with you. But--" I made myself sound confident. "You'll be okay, just fine."

And she was. They left a couple days later, grocer Puffin proudly driving them in his new Ford, glad of a reason to go somewhere and show off his new car--and make a few dollars.

Amy gave birth to Lillian May a week after they got to Seaside. Not much wiggle room in David's time-schedule. The baby was perfect, but Amy was too weak for the trip back until nearly a month later. Her labor turned out to be long and difficult. They'd been grateful for the medical assistance, and so was I. And in a silly, secret way, I felt superior.

When he got home David pulled the Smithers' family Bible from where they kept it in the top drawer of their bedroom chest and David added the birth of Lillian May to the chronicle.

Born to Amy and David Smithers
Lillian May Smithers
Seaside, Oregon January 25, 1920
Thanks be to God

24. THE LONELIEST WEEKS

*T*he five weeks they were gone were the loneliest weeks of my life. Worse even than the five months in the cabin, for then I'd had David at least once a day.

I popped corn, but it was tasteless. Sewing made me nervous. I worked on the Beach quilt and had it nearly finished. It was hard without someone to keep Sampson entertained while I sewed. I could only work on it when he was sleeping. I enjoyed it though, as it had all fit together much better than I had imagined. Somehow, working with the material, I felt closer to that time when I had first been getting to know David, as if that barely-bearable tension I'd felt then was somehow stitched into the design, into the material even.

The day came when I turned the last piece of the binding under, when I backstitched the last stitch, making a good knot. Then I embroidered my name in the left hand corner, on the sand:

The Beach in Winter
Sophie Elm
Cannon Beach. Feb. 1, 1920

I had a cup of tea and admired it, then took it to my bedroom and put in on my bed. Done.

I found the house too quiet at night, too lonely to stay up much after Sampson had gone to bed. When I got to bed it felt so big for just me. Some nights I'd give in when Sampson wanted to get in my bed, not his. It was comfort to us both. After a few days he stopped looking around so much for David and Amy. With the passing of time, I missed them even more, despite the fact that Sampson and I were really close during those weeks alone. He turned eleven months old while they were gone. Every day of his growing brought a new experience for both of us.

I established a new routine that met our needs better. We were more casual about things, such as waiting until evening before washing up the day's dishes. I was able to relax with my baby in a way I wasn't able to when I'd had chores to do with Amy. We sat together in ease while he nursed. I turned the chair to the window so we could look out at the ocean. It was peaceful as Sampson picked up my mood and nursed more quietly than his usual active way, watching with me as the ocean swelled and poured foam onto the shore.

But with no adults, the days were often lonely and boring. About once a week I'd walk up to Puffin's store, carrying Sam, to get basic foodstuffs but more to have someone to talk to. The trips to the store always unnerved me some. We'd told Puffin the same story I'd told the boys, that I was staying to housekeep and take care of David's wife during her pregnancy. He didn't see either Amy or me when I was in the last of my pregnancy but still I felt uncomfortable living under the sharp eyes of Puffin and his wife, Mrs. P.

They were used to seeing the four of us together and accepted the story that Sampson was Amy and David's child. I was nervous about going there with the baby even though we had told the Puffins that it was easier for all if Sampson stayed with me while they were in Seaside for the delivery. To that end I even bought milk from them for Sampson. They didn't know I used it to get him used to a cup but that his primary milk was from me.

The other reason to go to Puffin's store was to see if there were any messages or mail for me. There seldom was, but one day Amy's publisher sent finished copies of her first book, Sampson,

Boy of the Sea, and I wrote her immediately. She answered, ecstatic with the birth of her healthy daughter, and a book in the same year.

The weather again got on my nerves, but for a different reason. Now there was no one to watch Sampson when I went outside. He was walking around the furniture, flinging everything within reach to the floor. I thought he was going to drive me crazy. When he was awake I wanted him asleep and when he was sleeping the house was dead quiet and I wanted him awake. We fought over the bookcase. It fascinated him, I guess because, like a dog nuzzling old shoes when it's left alone, the books smelled of David and Amy. They played with them, so he did.

That's why I started reading. One night when Sampson went to bed early, tired after a day of chasing the cat around the house, wailing when I was outside and hanging on me when I was in. He'd made his usual mess. I was putting the books back in their place when I found Girl of the Limber lost from under the dining table.

The cover was wet where he'd chewed on the edges, so I left it on the table to dry. It was still there when I settled down to write Mom and Dad. I wrote them at least twice a month, telling them all about Amy's baby. I'd already explained about the new one coming, making it sound like I'd come home if I could, but Amy was such a weakling that I couldn't just yet.

Everything seemed too quiet, inside and out. It made me twitchy. The book just laid there, its chawed cover still dark from Sampson's four slurpy teeth. Looking at it, all I could think of was Amy and David sitting night after night reading by the fire. David often read out loud. I always wondered how they could sit like that, for hours sometimes. I was sure it'd drive me crazy.

But now, tonight, I was lonely for them, and like Sampson, the next best thing was their books.

I put more wood on the fire, partially just to hear the crackle, and settled down in David's chair with a thin quilt over my legs and a cup of hot tea on the little table beside his chair. I sat there for a while watching the flames, thinking over the last two years, until I couldn't stand thinking anymore and opened the book.

You must remember that I'd never read anything but the Bible, and only parts of that, and a few schoolbooks, history and such that I found boring. I took a while to get used to a story like that with no Chapter 1, Verse 3, or battles to remember. Once I got over feeling wasteful about spending time on reading, I got caught up in it. It took me a week or so to find out the girl was going to be all right, despite her crazy mother. And when I finished it I started another, about a strange boy. Little Shepherd of the Hills I think it was, and read that through. Then I started on Moby Dick but it was hard reading and I never did finish it, though David tried to get me to.

25. PRE-T-T-Y

*T*hey returned in the first week in April, David, Amy, and beautiful little Lillian.

As I said, about once a week Sampson and I walked into town, taking the steps David had cut into the hill behind the house up to the road. Cannon Beach wasn't much of a town, then, just a few buildings, plus the hotel. The store had a phone where David could call if he had any messages for me.

When I walked in, early that first week of April, both Sampson and I were cold from the mist. I sat down in the chair by the coal stove and unwrapped the baby. My arms were aching from carrying him. He was getting to be a big boy. It felt so good to sit down for a bit and just listen to Puffin's gossip. He didn't think it was gossip, of course. He told everyone who would listen that Mrs.

P. told everything she knew and a lot that she didn't and that was why he never told her the messages that came through the phone. It was a clear case of the pot calling the kettle black, although it did drive her mad that he never told her anything. He was tall and thin, spry. Mrs. P. was short and heavy, downright fat, though I hate to say it. I was there once when the phone rang. He nearly ran her over getting to it, being agile. Mrs. Puffin moved slow, and breathed hard if she tried to speed up any. He always beat her to the phone, no matter where he was.

Their name fit her. I always wondered what she was like when they got married, whether she had grown to fit the name or it was accidental. She was a good soul. When he told me about the baby she was as thrilled as I. The next time I came in she gave me a pink bonnet she'd made, trimmed with lace and embroidered with tiny roses, to give to Amy for Lillian.

Puffin liked to make his customers guess if there had been a call. "Well, hello," he'd always say when you came in. If there had been a message his voice would have an important I-have-a-secret tone that attracted your attention. It made you look at him curiously, which was what he wanted.

It irritated me that this self-important man would play with me so. If you got mad and said, "Okay, Puffin, out with it. Did somebody call?" he found something that needed doing in the back room. Make you wait.

"Mrs. P.," he'd call, "There's a customer out here for you." Since she knew less than you did about what message might have been left, the two of you would stumble around the subject, filling your order and awkwardly discussing the weather until he came back in, acting as if he'd suddenly remembered. "Oh, by the way, would you believe it?"

No.

I found it difficult this time to play his game.

"Mr. Puffin, have you heard from David?"

He narrowed his eyes at me and Mrs. Puffin tilted her head.

"You know," he said slowly, "that's interesting, you calling Smithers by his first name right out like that. I always thought... 'Course I never knew anybody before 'at had a housekeeper." His eyebrows and shoulders rose a bit to show his disapproval. "I always thought they was Mr. and Mrs. to their help, huh?"

I didn't react to his suggestion that I might be more than a

139

housekeeper, just sat quietly and looked at him calmly. I'm sure my eyes were flashing though, because Mrs. Puffin started clearing her throat and he stopped playing the cat and mouse game with me.

"Well, how'd you guess I'd heard from Smithers? Guess you figgered they'd be back soon, huh?"

I nodded.

"Well, well. You're right. Tomorrow in fact."

I started, my mouth opening with surprise.

"Surprised ya, huh? Me too. I'd thought he'd want me to come pick them up but he got some fella there with a big ol'-fashioned horse and buggy outfit who was coming over this way to visit his folks." He was obviously disappointed that he wouldn't get to show off his machine again.

"'Course I couldn't go now anyway. My busy time you know, people thinking about spring plantin' and all, and getting ready for summer visitors." He always called them visitors, never tourists.

Tomorrow! I bought sugar, flour and chocolate. Puffin had just got a ham in from one of the farms and I bought that, too. I walked home in a mind fog. Sampson seemed light, even with the groceries in my other arm.

I laughed about nothing and he laughed with me. I started humming when we were on a flat space on the path, and he started humming with me, singing with me. My heart just about burst right there, excited about wanting to share this latest trick of his with David. And Amy.

Sampson's little mouth moved around trying to make the same sounds I was, it was so cute. Oh, he was adorable. I couldn't wait for Amy and David to be back to share him with. I was so full of excitement, the waiting of the last weeks was about to be over. We could get back to normal living. I'd clean the house.

Sampson saw flowers beside the path and he pointed to them.

"Pret-t-y."

I about dropped him in the excitement of hearing his word.
They were the first spring flowers we'd seen and it was the first
word he said without prompting.

We stopped right there and picked them. Sampson clutched
them in his little fists all the way home. He bent the stems but I
knew David and Amy wouldn't care. I put them into a vase and
told Sampson, "Don't touch. For Daddy and Amy." And he didn't,
other than to just go up and touch the vase, and then look at me and
say, "Pret-ty? Da Da?"

I'd smile yes and he'd touch again with just the tip of his
finger.

He was probably as happy to see me happy and not yelling at
him as he was at the idea of Daddy and Amy. I don't think he knew
what was happening. Tomorrow didn't have much meaning to him,
but he responded to my joy with his own smiles. When he went
down for his afternoon nap he hummed himself to sleep.

I did love that boy.

26. DADDY'S SMILE

When they pulled up late the next afternoon I had the ham baked. Cornbread was keeping warm in the side oven. I was ready to heat some canned tomatoes from last summer's garden, and I had baked a three-layer chocolate cake. Everything was waiting, as were Sam and I.

I grabbed my little boy and stuffed him into his coat. He wrapped his arms and legs around me and we ran down the steps to meet them.

That's the day everything changed.

I can't blame Lily. She was only a baby, but she stole my David away from me.

I'd thought David was silly and daddy-proud when Sampson was born, but it was nothing compared to the way he made over that little girl.

When I saw him stepping from the buggy I thought my heart would bust. I hollered, "Hello! Welcome back."

He turned to see me running towards him. He only had to take a couple of steps before he threw his arms around both of us. He smelled and felt so good. With the buggy driver right there he couldn't kiss me, but after a long hug he took Sampson and kissed him hard, laughing all the time.

"It's so good to be back. And look at my little Sampson. So big. Look Amy, how big he is." And hugging him again he said, "Boy did we miss you both."

Not "I," but "We." I didn't notice the difference until later.

Amy called from within the coach, laughter in her voice, "Sophie! David! Help us out."

I went to the door and Amy handed me a bundle of warm baby. Lily was so wrapped up against the cold that I only saw a bit of her pink face through the opening in the blanket. David helped Amy out, one arm tight around Sampson, who, frightened by all the noise, was squirming to get back to me.

Amy kissed me on the cheek and squeezed me, "Oh, Soph, I'm so glad to be here. We thought that ride would never end. I can't wait to get into the house. I'm so tired."

She looked wonderful to me, though her face was pale. Her hair was cut in a new style, curling softly around the edges of a new cap that fit close to her head. Her eyes sparkled as she smoothed the bundle I held. "We've got to get her inside so I can show you our treasure." Looking at Sampson, she said, "I've got some huggin' and squeezin' to do."

Within a short time we had babies, adults, boxes and trunks moved down into the house. As soon as the door shut and we were all alone Amy took the baby and, laying her gently on the table, unwrapped the blankets, untied her knit cap, and lifted her gently to me.

"Lillian May, meet your Auntie Sophie."

I looked down into a face that was baby beautiful. Like Sampson, she had hair. but it was blond. Curly hair, like Amy's. Little curls brushed her tiny face that was the color of rich cream. She had bright rosy cheeks, but it was her eyes that were amazing.

"Look, Sophie," crowed David. "Amy's grandmother had violet eyes and I think Lily will too." He sounded like this was some special talent that he could take credit for.

"Here." He took the baby from me. "Watch this." He rocked her slowly up and down and tickled her under her chin. "Daddy's little dumpling going to smile for Aunt Sophie?"

Her mouth twitched. She had David's mouth, and it spread out into David's big grin but with tiny dimples at the corners. Daddy's smile. He was too satisfied with himself. "Ain't she a corker?"

But now the smile faded into a frown and she started crying.

"Oh oh, Momma. I think our girl's hungry."

I settled Amy into her chair with her feet on the cushioned stool. David handed Lillian over. Amy unbuttoned the top of her dress and David watched with intense interest until the baby found the nipple, stopped crying and started sucking.

"There," he said, as if he'd done it himself, "Lily May sure knows where dinner is."

After dinner for everyone was over--David didn't comment on the special cake, but Amy did--we sat around the table. They, David mostly, told me all about Lillian's birth.

There'd been no special problem, just a very long labor, over twenty hours, which David threatened to repeat in length and detail.

Amy interrupted him. "But it was worth it. I'd gladly go through it again, twice so, except..."

There was a short silence during which I looked from one to the other, wondering.

David closed it. "Right after she was born, as soon as it was decent, according to the nurse, I went in and... Well, it's just a shame you weren't there. Amy was holding Lily and looking more

144

beautiful than ever, if that's possible." He looked at her, she beamed at him.

I felt like an intruder.

He continued on with detail after detail of Lillian's first weeks, her first feeding, her first bath, how she slept so quietly that it frightened him, on and on. At last Amy, sounding exhausted, said "David, I simply must go to bed."

We helped Amy and the baby upstairs. David put Lily in the cradle he'd made for Sampson and that I'd prepared before they came home. While he settled them I put Sampson to sleep in the small bed David had bought from a neighboring farmer, through Puffin.

Tired from the trip both Amy and the baby went to sleep quickly. David hovered around Lily a while to make sure she was okay, 'til I laughed and said, "Come on, she'll be just fine. Let the poor babe sleep in peace. You're worse than a brand-new mother hen."

He grinned that proud grin. "Yeah, I guess so, but ain't she fine?" he whispered as we went downstairs.

Frankly, I could hardly wait to get downstairs. I wanted to be alone with him. Wanted very much to be alone with him.

He still hadn't kissed me. I was tired of waiting, so, before he could start unpacking or doing something else, I grabbed him and kissed him. He seemed surprised. I was seldom aggressive.

But he didn't resist. He moaned until he made me stop.

That was a switch. I was confused and my feelings were hurt.

"I think we'd better take a walk," he said. He wasn't acting like my David. Was there something wrong with me? Or him?

I put on my heavy, hooded jacket as he got the gas lantern from the hook by the door. He put his sou'wester on and lit the lamp. His hands were unsteady, he had difficulty holding the match still.

I followed him out. We picked our way carefully down the path. At the steep, tricky part at the end, he handed me the lantern, felt his way carefully. When he got to the bottom, he took the lamp to set on the sand and held out his arms.

I nearly knocked him over wrapping my arms around him. He wasn't a big man but he stood strong, caught me and held me so tight I had to loosen his grip to breathe.

We left the lantern wedged between rocks near the path and walked. He took my right hand in his left and put them both deep in his coat pocket. We walked like that for a long time, along the water line with only pale moonlight to show the way.

The roar of the surf and a harsh wind swept away the questions I cried aloud. "What's the matter, David? Don't you care anymore?"

I didn't dare say "love." What if he said, "No?" Besides, his kisses were more loving than ever, so that couldn't be it. It couldn't.

My questions went unanswered, as if he didn't hear.

Finally he turned and ran his fingers across my lips, gently, to silence me. We walked for a long ways before he veered off the low tide to a sheltered place along the bank. We sat down on the damp sand and held each other without speaking.

I began to get angry. He was acting so strange, yet not at all like a man who had quit loving.

"Okay, David, what is it? What the hell's the matter with you?" I always could swear easier in the dark.

"Nothing's the matter. You don't have to be mean about it."

Now he was offended.

I ignored his complaint. "I just would like an explanation, that's all. One minute you're hot, the next cold. What's going on?"

"Well, Sophie. To be truthful..."

I wanted all of that.

"I don't mean to have more children."

"What?" I wasn't sure I'd heard right.

"Sophie," he pleaded. "Listen, please. For twelve years I had one wife and no children and now all at once I have two wiv-- Well, I have both you and Amy, and now Sampson and Lillian." He threw his hands up from my shoulder. "It's enough," he said, so quietly I had to lean closer to hear his words.

That was all. He didn't want any more kids, so we couldn't-- But surely there was a way-- "Sampson is almost a year old and we've... I'm not pregnant, so--"

"Don't be stupid. Can't you see how foolish we've been? There's only one sure way...when people don't want any more children...well, they don't. That's all. They stop."

I knew better than that. I couldn't believe he was so ignorant, "David, there are ways." I didn't know what they were but I expected he could find out. It wasn't my place. After all, he was older, certainly more experienced. And I was a woman. An unmarried woman. Where was I to go to find out?

"Sure, there are ways, but I'm not taking any chances right now. The doctor told me Amy shouldn't have any more children. When I asked how, he just said to leave her alone for a few months, then come see him late this summer and he'd tell me what we could do.

"If Amy and I can't... I don't think you and I...should. It wouldn't be right."

"But, what about me? You didn't think about how to not get

me pregnant?" He hadn't demanded an answer right then, because he hadn't thought about me, at all.

"I couldn't."

He wasn't giving me a choice. The responsibility of being a minister's son always fell on him at the wrong time.

"Well, I'm sure glad you didn't seem over-anxious." I stood up, brushing the damp sand from my clothes.
He jumped up. "But, I still love you as much as ever.

Nothing's changed."
I looked at him.
"Well, a little. But, I'll fix it, you'll see." He tried to laugh.

"After all, bigger men than I--"
He stopped when I started laughing.
He went to bed with Amy that night and the next night he was back with me but I found his closeness almost worse than when he wasn't there. Now I was willing, even with Amy in the next room. But he wasn't. It just didn't seem fair.

27. A LONG NARROW BOX

*T*he room was dark and chilly with only coals from the fire sending a red glow into the room. I looked at Aunt Sophie who was getting up slowly.

"We're going to have to put some more wood on that fire. Got those berries done just in time." She went to the window and pulled the curtain aside.

"It's starting to rain." She ran her hand slowly back over her head, then brushed down the front of her dress and apron, as if wiping away old memories. "Been dry too long anyway, I like to see it rain."

She turned on a light over a small table in the corner. The table with the drawer that no children could get into. She always told us, "I keep my private things in there. If you don't get into my things I won't get into yours."

Aunt Sophie could be real nasty if we got into her pocketbook, or opened her mail, so we learned not to. And we could trust her not to pry into our lives either. Consequently we told her many things we couldn't tell our parents, and left things at her house we didn't want them to see.

She pulled the drawer open slowly, her hands trembling with

fatigue and emotion. Taking out a long, narrow box, she set it on the table. She felt under the drawer until she found the key that was taped to the underside. She pulled it loose. Slowly, her hands more steady, she unlocked the box, lifted the lid and started to reach into it. But then she put the lid down and walked slowly across the room, to me.

She put the box in my hands. "Here, you look through it if you want to. I'm going to bed."

There were lines in her face that I'd not seen before. She looked old, and sad. I was seeing her for the first time as the adult she now trusted I was.

"I'm too old, and tired. It was all a long time ago. I don't know if I even care anymore."

I wanted to say, "You brought it up."

I didn't. I just held the box, feeling the comfortable weight in my hands.

She went into her bedroom off the living room.

Leaving the box on my chair, I added some wood to the fire and went into the kitchen to make some instant cocoa. When I got back her door was closed. No light showed underneath so I settled with the box into the familiar old chair.

28. BRITTLE, YELLOWED LETTERS

*T*he pungent fragrance of cedar wood was strong when I opened the box. In a neat stack lay a collection of old newspaper clippings and letters, the painful record of love gone awry. Only a few items appeared to have been handled much. I'd guess the others were simply put away and not touched again, being the kinds of things it is difficult to keep, but impossible to throw in the trash.

I read the papers as I came to them, in the order they'd been placed in the box.

> DAVID SMITHERS died at his home in Cannon Beach yesterday, August 23, 1964. He was born in Natural Bridge, Va., July 20, 1884. He was preceded in death by Amy Smithers, his wife of 57 years, July 12, 1964. Mr. Smithers was a well known artist who had resided in Cannon Beach for many years. He is survived by son Jonathan S. Smithers, of Cannon Beach and daughter Lillian M. Lawnrose of Laramie, Wy.; by grandchildren Davie Smithers of Damascus, Or., and Gregory and Jennifer Lawnrose of Depoe Bay, Or. and great grandchildren Amy and Alica Smithers, Damascus, Or. Funeral arrangements are pending.

I put David's obituary aside and picked up the next paper. It was Amy's death notice, in July 1964, listing the same survivors. Had David died because without her there was no longer a reason to live?

Perhaps. I wondered. No cause of death was listed for either.

I wondered too about their house. Was it still there or had it been torn down to make way for an A-frame, or more likely, turned into a Gift Shoppe of Unusual and Rare Items From the Sea, with parking space behind the building? Asphalt where Sophie's cabin had been?

I looked at the next item, an envelope.

It held a letter from Sophie's son, written at sea, the date placing it during World War II. It appeared to have been opened only once and then put back. The pages were fresh, the pencil writing clear and unsmudged.

On one of Uncle Sam's ships headed for only the Brass knows where.

> Dear Mother,
>   It seems strange to call someone besides Mother Amy as Mother, but you are my mother, so I will. This whole letter might seem strange to you, after so many years of not hearing from me but I've seen some bad things in this war and it seems to me if I can only make one thing right in this world at least that's one less wrong, and maybe every little bit helps. I hope so.
>
>   I'm writing about that letter I wrote to you on my 14th birthday. I'm sorry. I didn't mean it. I guess I meant it at the time but I'm older now and I hope not so stupid. Dad and Mom don't know what I said, they thought it was the usual thank-you note. When I come back, if I come back, I've seen some awful things and sometimes a person gets scared, but, when I come back I want to come see you. Would that be all right with you? I would just like

to see you and talk with you for awhile.

Well, I've got to go now. Wherever we are going it must be important. The Brass is closed mouthed but we have our ideas. I will probably be all right. I've been lucky so far.

Please write soon if you would like to see me. Even if that's not possible I would like to hear from you.

Love,
Jon S.

There were no later letters from him. No clue as to whether she'd replied, or not.

I set the mail aside and drank my cold cocoa, staring into the flames of Sophie's stove. I sat there for a while before opening the next letter. It was from Jon, the one he'd written at fourteen.

April 4, 1933
To Miss Elm,
As you can see it's my birthday. I'm 14 years old now. Do you care? Don't think that just because you send me a card and some money once a year that I care anything about you! If you really cared about me you would come see me. You could at least send a present but I guess it's too much trouble for you to find out what a 14 year old boy likes and it's certainly too much trouble to write and ask me. But I guess you are too busy. I wouldn't write back anyway.

Probably you just don't care, so I don't either! Do not send me any more money! Just forget about me like I have forgotten about you. I have my own Mother, and Father to give me money. They love me to. But you don't know about that because you are just a phony mother.

Don't send me any more cards either.

    Your ex-son
    Jon S. Smithers

Children have a good sense of where to hit to hurt--near the same place where they feel their own pain. I was relieved to see that the next envelope was a Christmas card signed, "All our love, David, Amy, Sampson and Lily."

Written on the back was simply:

Hoping you are well. We are all fine here, we are very busy. Found these photographs, thought you might like to have them. Love, Amy

p.s. I took the one of David and the children last summer on the beach, the other we had taken when David sold a painting a few years back of some tourists (should I say 'summer visitor's?'? ha ha) poking around the tide pools at Haystack. Between my books and David's paintings we sell enuf to keep body and soul together and once in a while do something special, thus the studio photograph. --Amy

The pictures and the last two envelopes all looked as if they'd been handled often, yellowed and finger marked. I searched the photos closely. The studio photo revealed little of the personalities of the people, only that they were all very attractive. The photos had been studio tinted, giving them a liveliness not in most black and whites of the time. Amy looked more stern than Aunt Sophie had described her, but then so do most photos from that time. She looked contented, secure. Her eyes were clear and looked directly into the camera. David appeared to be a normally attractive man with interesting bushy eyebrows that Aunt Sophie had never talked about. Maybe they had gotten bushy with age. His eyes had a twinkle that came through the photo and caught my attention.

As they had for Sophie.

The children were young, probably eight and nine or so; they were childishly attractive. Sampson resembled his father but had the black, black hair of Aunt Sophie's youth.

The other was more revealing of their personalities. The three of them wore bathing suits, mid-30's style I'd guess. David stood in the middle holding a beach ball high in the air and the children on either side were reaching to grab it. Though obviously posed as all three were looking into the camera, their casual attitudes revealed more than a studio seriousness. All were grinning broadly. I stared at David. His hair was wild about his head, his face was tanned and his grin was heart-stopping--and he was at least fifty by then. Jon and Lily looked like him, full of fun, but fresh, eager. Lily had long blonde braids, brown eyes, and a perfect figure. Jon was no taller than his dad but more muscular, and he still had the black curly hair that marked him as Aunt Sophie's. Most remarkable was the full, good-natured intelligence shared by the trio and caught by the camera.

I finally put the pictures back in the card and added them to the pile. There were only two envelopes left. The first was another letter from Jonathan Sampson when he was only seven.

April 4, 1926
Dear Mommy Sofie,
     How aur you? I am fin. Mommy show me yur pixure toda Daddy drew me an you wen i was a babi. Mommy say i growed in yur timi. Thats funni! Mommy say you luv me. i luv you to. i in skool now. Secon grad. Mommy say i spel awfl. Daddy say i to smart! Well, got to go now. Mabe i see you ths sumr. i 7 yers old toda. Thank your four car and too dolar.

Luv
JONATHAN SAMPSON SMITHERS

155

Last, and explaining much, was a letter from David.

October 12, 1921

My dearest Sophie,
    It's been over a year now since you left and I still miss you terribly, especially when the sea is stormy and I walk lonely on the beach. Amy comes sometimes but with the children it is hard for us both to get out together. Getting them to sleep at the same time is hard. They both sleep in your old room and when it's daytime they just keep jabbering at each other and won't take their naps until we put one of them in our bed. And when they do sleep and we go out, Amy is nervous the whole time that they will wake up and fall down the stairs or something so we don't get many walks alone.

    Love, are you ever coming back? I didn't believe you when you said you wouldn't return but it's been so long. You can't know how much I miss you or you wouldn't stay away. Surely you would be happier with us than with your sister. If you want children to take care of we certainly have them here! Sampson kept looking for you after you left. And so did I. My heart aches with wanting you. Are you still making your beautiful quilts? The Haystack one is on our bed now and Amy often says how lovely it is and how nice it makes the room look and wants you to know we are taking good care of it.

    It's cloudy and stormy today. One of the kind you didn't like too much but that I like best. Sampson is well. He had a couple of colds last winter but that's all. He is talking up a storm and we have to watch him all the time he is awake or he is out the door and down the hill to the water. But don't worry, we put a lock high up on the door so he can't do that anymore!

    We take L.M. with us to Puffin's and I think she's

helping our credit there. Puffin is as proud of her as if he had done more than just drive her mother to Seaside!

Amy says to say hello and tell you to come visit anytime. She means come back soon, like I do. She is working now on a story about a little girl named L.M. (guess who) who travels about the world with her parents and has a special affinity for communication with dogs and cats which of course leads her into all sorts of adventures. Amy hopes to work it into a series like the Sampson books. Please write us and tell us how you are. If you can't come now at least let us know how you are doing. Miss you awfully!

All my love, David

I read the letter twice. I didn't know whether Aunt Sophie had answered but since none of the other letters had any reference to seeing her, and there were no other letters from David I guessed he'd failed to win her back with emotional calls.

How strong she was. Or was it just stubbornness? I knew from the way she looked and sounded when she talked of him that her love had not died. Nor had her love for her baby left her. So what had she done with it?

That answer I knew. It had gone to Boyd most directly, and to the others of us who were rocked in her arms and warmed in her bed and listened to when we had long complicated dreams and stories to tell. And later on, our loves were brought before her, the pain and joy shared in return for a soft shoulder or a sharp comment that we resented at the time but that would come back in the dead of night and focus our own questions on his, or her, or our, actions. Once we married though, her advice and soft shoulder disappeared. In fact, if she voiced an opinion at all it was in favor of the other person.

"I think you could perhaps try patience. You've never been very patient. Now that you're an adult it's way past time you stopped thinking of yourself so much."

With advice like that we soon stopped asking. After all it was obvious she didn't know what she was talking about. She'd never been married.

As far as we knew she had never even been in love. We teased her to find out but she would only say, "There's some things for me to know and you to wonder about."

I wasn't married yet, but I planned to be soon. I knew Aunt Sophie didn't approve of Len. She worried about his temper. We argued constantly about every little thing and he didn't like my new job either. Since we were going to be married why did I need a career? She warned that a possessive man before marriage can become even more jealous after the vows are taken, and...

I'd stopped talking to her about him. She'd never been in love. She didn't know how his eyes, his hands, and his concern about me made me feel.

Now, in the dark, I wondered at her reason for exposing her story, the deep self she'd kept hidden all these years. Why to me, now? Sure, I'd always listened better than the other cousins to her stories and had spent more time with her, but there was more to it than that.

I decided to think about it tomorrow after I left. Right now I was going to put on a couple more pieces of wood to the fire, close it up, and go to bed. But first I put everything back in the box, locked it and returned it to its place in the drawer and left the key on the table.

There was the boy to have the answer about tomorrow, too. Cannon Beach? Could it be that he still lived there? He would be old, impossibly old. An old boy? As much as the answers intrigued me, I dreaded asking her the question. I didn't want Sampson to be old, but neither did I want him to be dead.

29. NO ESCAPE

*T*he next morning dawned bright and clear. Sun through the kitchen window reflected off the chrome edging of the table. The key was gone.

Perhaps we could forget the whole thing. She had left them all and I was sure the reason could be applied to my situation in some oblique way. Why else had she told me her story? Almost everyone was dead and gone. It was morbid to rehash old wounds. What happened fifty years ago couldn't have any relevance to me.

Now, with my senses alert to a reason behind the telling, I was eager to be gone. I was not going to listen to unwanted advice, however indirect. I'd just grab a cup of coffee and be gone.

But she was quicker than I. "Well, good morning, sleepyhead." It wasn't even seven o'clock yet.

Before I could finish saying, "Just a cup of coffee please, I've got to run," she was at the stove.

"Get some bacon and eggs into you and then I have a favor to ask before you go."

"Well, Aunt So," I hedged, "I just wanted to get some coffee--"

"Nonsense. You need more than coffee. I'll make you a good breakfast."

I kept quiet. She was herself again, full of energy and hustle, not the old woman I'd seen the night before.

"Now, if after breakfast you could stay for awhile and help me with these windows, I'd sure appreciate it."

"The windows? But you always told me not to wash them when the sun is shining on them 'cause they streak."
"That was when I didn't need any help and could wait until a cloudy day. But..." She bent her head to look feeble, "When a strong body that can reach up, and isn't afraid of breaking old bones from falling off a chair comes around, I just have to grab it and make use of it. "

I was wearing short sleeves. She laughed and squeezed the muscles in my right arm. Her fingers were softly rough, a contradiction but there she was, defined by the feel of her skin. She was pulling out all the stops again so I gave in. After all, maybe she was telling the truth.

"You know," she said, as she put the coffee in front of me, "I always did like clean windows."

I'd never particularly noticed it.

"In fact I was washing windows the day I decided to leave."

There it was. She was going to continue with the story despite the fact I'd not brought it up.

30. NIGHTMARE

When they brought Lily home I was so happy to have them back. I laughed and teased David about his obsession with the child. But the problem wasn't him. It was in me, and in the situation. I was possessive and jealous, not unlike your Len.

Aha! This reference to him confirmed my suspicions. She questioned his character.

Before Lily came, Sampson was the center of our attention. We all loved him, but because I'd given him to David, I felt we had a special closeness. I never saw resentment in Amy of that closeness. She accepted it, with an occasional envy that I saw now and then, but she wasn't mean-spirited. She seemed as happy for David as he was. But their baby brought a change to our lives.

David paid more attention to Lily and Amy than he did to Sampson and me. I was still nursing Sampson, but David didn't crowd around and crow over us anymore. Now it was Lily and Amy who got this attention.

Then Lily got the colic. Sampson had never been sick a day in his short life, so when Lily cried in pain David couldn't stand it. For weeks he walked the floor with her at night. He wouldn't let Amy or me do it.

"You have enough to do in the day taking care of these babies," he said. "I'll take care of Lily at night. You both need your rest. You can't get worn down."

Her crying and the long nights were exhausting for all of us. Even through my sleep I could hear her when she woke up and started crying.

During the day we were all tired, but only my temper got short. They'd waited so long for a baby, no sacrifice was too tiring for them. Amy kept saying, "This will pass. We just have to wait it out. Think of poor Lily. It's harder on her than us."

I wasn't sure. They were spoiling her terribly, but I said nothing.

Somewhere in her fourth month Lily's colic eased, but it was already too late for me. Probably if it hadn't been that straw it would have been something else. I couldn't share someone so close to my heart. Amy and David could, but I couldn't. They had each other and Lily in a way that would never include me. I wanted David and Sampson to be all mine. To care mostly about me.

That was never going to happen. David was a good talker. He'd convinced me this could work for all of us, but the reality was that it worked well for him--and Amy too in some ways. Would she have Lily if not for me and Sampson?

I was extra. I wasn't needed. David had manipulated me. I knew I had to take some responsibility too. I'd gone along with David's scheme because it was the only way I could get what I wanted: David. I kept my thoughts to myself but inside I seethed with anger and tears.

I couldn't take my frustration out on Lily--she was so tiny--or Amy or David--I was too afraid of losing him. So I took it out on the one person I had who was mine. Sampson.

I decided he was going to be potty trained and weaned. And that he'd stop pulling things from tables and bookshelves. And would mind my every word. He was going to be a perfect little man.

He wasn't ready for the sudden change, and my anger toward him made it worse. You would think my experience with Mandy's kids would have taught me that children move slowly or quickly according to their own pace. Forcing your schedule on them, it seldom works. But they'd been Mandy's children, not mine. I'd had to accept doing things her way which, since we had the same upbringing, was not all that different from mine. But I saw things that I would do different if they were mine. I wouldn't have put up with half the nonsense she did.

The difference was that she had four little ones close together. I had only one. He was all mine, and now my full attention went to him.

When he wet his pants I spanked him and shamed him. "You big baby! Naughty dirty boy!"

"He's only a baby," Amy said, almost crying.

David just looked at me and took Sampson away, holding him on his lap and rocking him. "It's all right. You'll do better next time."

Sampson not only didn't do better next time, he got worse. He started wetting the bed again, something he hadn't done since he was about a year old. I put him back in night diapers, which he fought because I shamed him so about it. "No, no," he'd cry, trying to wiggle away.

It got to the point where only Amy could put him to bed because he ran away from me.

Weaning him was awful, too. If I'd just eased into it, he might have given in, but one morning as he started to climb into my lap I just said, "No, you're a big boy now. Eggs and cereal and a cup for you."

He fought it. He threw up. He knocked the cup to the floor and reached for me. Soon that didn't work because there was nothing there. At first my breasts swelled and hurt, and I'd say--I remember it and am ashamed--"This hurts me more than you. You hurt Mommy."

David got very angry when I said that. "You have no right. Can't you see what you're doing to him? What is the matter with you?"

"Don't interfere. He's mine. You take care of Lily, I'll take care of Sampson."

I didn't look at his face when he said, "He doesn't belong to anyone. He is his own."

Thus I brought screaming and crying to what had been a peaceful house. The matter with me was that I was blind jealous. The sharing didn't work for me. Maybe it would of if I'd been brought up to it, but I wasn't.

It didn't work for me in our little Cannon Beach family.

As long as I, through Sampson, was the primary recipient of David's attention I was happy. Only I had been able to provide him with a child. But now I had to share this glory, and be happy about it. It wasn't in me.

When it comes to our own child most of us are blind. The child must be perfect. We all go about trying to make perfect children in our different ways. One believes in the belt, another in a kiss, another counsels a mixture between the two. Perhaps one method will work, but when you have three people, three ways in conflict, the mixture doesn't work.

It certainly didn't work with Sampson. He became impossible. Now we had two crying babies, and three exhausted, tense, and angry adults.

Maybe if I'd still had David's physical love I'd have been different, but it was gone. Even the hugs and kisses disappeared.

I grew more frantic in my determination to make Sampson a perfect child. I needed, wanted, David's approval of our son, our specialness. I was jealous of Amy and her power with David, her life with him before I came, and now, with Lily as their focus.

I don't know what was worse, my scattergun anger, my jealousy, or that all the gentle love play with David dried up.

There were many nights when he didn't come to my bed at all. His excuse at first was that he had to be up with Lily. When he was there, the intimacy wasn't. Always, I thought, tomorrow night... But it didn't happen.

There was something else, something I didn't see until later. Always I'd made quilts, as my sisters did, but with me it had been more. An obsession almost. Where my sisters sewed out of duty and need, to me it was a joy.

With David and Amy's appreciation my stitching took on a new meaning. I was an artist. Creative.

Caring for Sampson, and Amy and Lily, left me no time or energy for quilting. The scrap bag by my bed was in the way. I stumbled over it and Sam got into it. I shoved it under the bed. Once in a while I'd sweep under there and hit the bag, making the dust fly.

Nothing but babies.

I loved babies, but...

In my confusion I looked for someone to blame. Everything wrong must be because of baby Lily. I didn't blame her, I told myself in my lonely bed--just as lonely when David was in it now as when he wasn't--but before she came... If she hadn't come...

If she hadn't been born...

If she went away...

My thoughts stopped there, guiltily.

And then I got a letter from my sister Lydia. Her twin, Lucy, was getting married in September. Lucy and Jack were planning a honeymoon at the beach in Seaside. Did I know a nice place they could stay in Cannon Beach for a couple of days?

I wasn't sure whether this was a thin excuse to get me to invite them to stay over with us. I could easily sidestep that. It wasn't my house. They thought I was the housemaid who took care of the kids.

I read and re-read the letter until the sweat on my hands smudged Lydia's neat writing. I put the letter away in my bedroom drawer where I wouldn't be running into it.

I didn't like the idea of Lucy being there at all. I didn't know this Jack, but Lucy was sharp-eyed and sharp-tongued. It would be impossible to explain why Sampson called me Mommy, and he looked too much like me for comfort.

One morning in early August I was thinking about how impossible Sampson had become. I was washing the living room window that opened to the sea and watching a couple walking arm in arm on the beach. It was windy and they were snuggled close together. My heart hurt to see them. The pail of water was by my feet. Sampson walked over and deliberately, I'm sure of it, pushed it over.

I jumped, and would have slapped him if the shock of the warm water on my feet hadn't triggered a memory. The water and the couple on the beach revived a fragment of the nightmare I'd had the night before and forgotten by morning.

In the dream I was walking out into the ocean, carrying a baby, Sampson. He was wrapped in a partially finished quilt. The waves didn't get us wet. I wasn't cold. It was very peaceful. Without warning a huge wave swept over us. When it was gone so was the baby, but not the quilt. I looked frantically for Sampson, but I couldn't find him, I ran back to the house, screaming, "David! David! Sampson's gone."

He looked at me oddly and said, "No he's not. He's right here." And there he was, smiling and cheerful playing on the rug.

"Well, then, where's Lily?"

"Lily?" he said. "Who's Lily?"

"I guess it was Lily I lost," I said, "but that's all right, because now we'll all be happy again."

Amy came up and kissed me on the cheek. "You're probably right, but it was an awful thing you did."

I smiled and let the quilt float down to cover Sampson.

That was all I remembered but it was enough make me know... I was wishing the baby dead. And Sampson gone? Right then I made my decision. I had to go away.

It would also solve the problem of what to do about Lucy and Jack.

I could see from the relief on David's and Amy's faces what they had feared I'd do to Sampson for dumping the pail over. Instead I just got the mop and cleaned up.

The sooner I left, the better. I decided just that quick. When I'd come to the point of wishing a child dead, perhaps both of them, I knew it was all wrong.

They were still watching me as I put the mop away. We were all quiet, even Sampson. I think Amy sensed it. My face always betrayed me.

"I have to leave." I didn't know how else to say it. There was no sense edging around it.

David was the first to react. Maybe Amy was waiting to take her cue from him, to see what he wanted.

"What are you talking about? You mean go away?" But he knew what I meant. And there was no conviction in his voice. I think he was relieved.

"Here. And now." Maybe I'd hoped for pleading, tears. If he'd begged me to stay, maybe... But he didn't.

Amy came over and put her arms around me. "Sophie, it's not necessary. Give it a few days thought. You'll see I'm right." For the second time I saw the look of sadness I'd seen only once before, the night she took me into her home. I was surprised, for I would not have done the same in her place. Yes, I think of her as Saint Amy.

"No. I've got to do this. I can't go on."

"It's been all right," David protested. "True, it has been a little rough lately." He defended. his position.

I raised my eyebrows. He could have said, "You've been rough," but he didn't. I knew and so did they.

"Maybe it's been all right for you and Amy, but not for me."

He started to protest but I stopped him. I shook my head and put my hand against his mouth. "I just can't do it. I tried." I looked from him to Amy. "We tried. And it didn't work." I moved towards Amy, but the look on her face stopped me.

Her eyes were guarded, her jaw firm and fierce. Fear. She swallowed, and stepped towards me.

It was odd, but what I noticed just then was the sound of the wind moving through the trees outside the window. Moving through us as well.

"What about Sampson?"

I knew the answer to that. I'd always known it, from the first time I saw her holding him. She loved him as much as I did, perhaps more, differently. The only way I could keep my vow to protect him was to give him up. She would be a better mother to him.

"Sampson will be just fine. Here. With you."

"Sophie." She came to me now, her eyes and face softening,
"Be sure. Are you sure you want this? Are you sure you know
what you're doing?"

"I know. It doesn't matter that I wish it were different. I joined
into this arrangement against my better judgment. You can give
him what I can't--two parents. At home he'd be considered a... You
know."

David winced.

"People here think he's yours and my people think so too. It
would only make things terrible for him if I took him with me.
Please understand."

Amy didn't understand. She struggled to keep a neutral face
but the tightness around her eyes and face relaxed. She would
never understand, but she agreed to my decision. Was glad of it.
Sampson was hers too. I don't think Amy would have ever left her
child, which was why I felt safe leaving him with her.

That doesn't mean I think I made the wrong choice. It was the
right one for Sampson. At that moment, that was what I cared
about. Circumstances are different for everyone. In our case it
would have hurt him more to take him with me into a world that
would never have seen him as I did. Today things are different, and
maybe I'd do different, but I don't know. Water under the bridge.

31. "YOU'LL BE BACK."

*A*my helped me pack. I didn't take much besides my clothes, some shells, Sampson's booties I'd made before he was born, and my scrap bag.

David went into town and arranged a ride for me with a couple who were going over to Seaside, where I could catch the train to Portland. When he came back I was ready. Amy came downstairs with the Beach quilt.

"Sophie. You forgot this."

"No. It's Sampson's. Keep it. Maybe he'll want it someday.
Tell him you got it from a lady who helped take care of him when he was a baby."

"I'll do no such thing. How, pray tell, would we explain you to Sampson when you come back?"

"I won't be back."

"Sure you will," David spoke up, turning from the door where he was setting my trunk and boxes before carrying them up to the road where the Seaside people were picking me up. "As soon as you get to Portland you'll realize your mistake. When you do, I want you to come right back." He'd clearly decided to act as if the whole thing was just a temporary situation, that when I came back I'd be fine again and so would everything else. Whether he really believed that or not...

For a bright man he was good at deceiving himself. And me, for a while.

A horn honked from up the hill. Mercifully, the children were asleep. I went upstairs while David and Amy carried my baggage up the hill.

Baby Lily was lying beside Sampson, her feet jammed into his back. I straightened her out, moving my hands against her legs ever so softly. She stirred slightly. I kissed her forehead, "I'm sorry little one."

Sampson was hard to leave. I didn't know if I could. I tucked the light blanket up around his shoulders and felt the little muscles in his arms. I tugged at his hair on his forehead, smoothed it. My hand traced his face, ran under his chin. I wiped off the bit of little-boy slobber that was there, wiped it on my shoulder. I leaned over quickly and kissed the back of his warm neck; I can taste it today, salty. "Goodbye little love. Son. My little Sampson. Be happy."

Blindly I got out of the house and wiped the tears away before I got to the car. But they started again. I hugged Amy hard. She had tears, too. "Good luck, dear Sophie."

And then, despite the couple who were watching all this with big eyes, I threw myself in David's arms and kissed him wildly. "David. I loved you so much."

"Please come back, Sophie. Please." He held me tight. "I love you too."

I got in the back seat as quickly as I could, a curtain of tears between me and them.

"Please, let's go now." I was sobbing. It was terribly embarrassing, crying in front of strangers.

We left.

It took forever to get to Seaside. The couple gave up trying to
have a conversation with me. They were kind. She patted my
shoulder. He helped me with my ticket and with getting onto the
train. I barely know how it was done.

I sat alone looking at the different greens and shapes of trees
as we passed through the forests. The train was slow; nevertheless,
I was in the Portland station before I was ready. Would I have ever
been ready?

Before getting on the streetcar, I called Mandy in Gresham to
have Zed meet me when I got off. They were glad to have me back
because Mandy was about due with Boyd. We had our hands full,
what with all the kids, and the canning and the new baby, and such.

I've been here most ever since, but a part of my heart has
always been in the fog and mist of the coast, with my other family.

32. SOME THINGS TO REMEMBER

*A*unt Sophie said, with no particular emotion in her voice, as if she hadn't just been telling me that extraordinary story, "And now you better be on your way or you'll be late." She walked me to my car.

"Wait," I said after I hugged her. "Did you ever regret it? Did you ever go back, see them, see Sampson, or David, or Amy?"

"Of course I regretted it." She looked away, but simply, as if examining a dying rose bush. "Almost as soon as I got to Mandy's, as David said I would. I missed Sampson terribly. I worried constantly, for a long time. Whenever a letter came I feared something might have happened, and when I didn't hear, it worried me even more.

"I suffered terribly. You can't imagine. There was no one to talk to. I had to hold it all in, pretend everything was perfectly normal. But at night when everyone was asleep I tormented myself, asking whether what I did was right or wrong. Whether I'd wronged Sampson. That guilt was the hardest to live with."

She looked at me clearly, directly. "No, I never went back. I had enough to do here, and after I waited a few months... It would have interrupted too many lives."

"But the cards, the letters?"

"Oh, at first I wrote often and they wrote back, and then, oh we wrote at Christmas time, like people do. You saw the letters. Too much hurt."

She opened the car door for me. "There is a little more to tell, and I think you want to know."

"About Sampson?"

"Yes, but now you've got to be on your way." She was now very anxious to close it and have me gone. I put my hand on the door to hold it open.

"Tonight, I have free time after I get off work. I won't be able to sleep unless you tell me. He's my cousin. Tonight after work? I'll pick something up from the grocery and feed you dinner, okay?"

"All right. But don't worry about dinner. I'll make that stew that you like."

At that I let her close the door. I rolled down the window. "I'll pick up some bread. You've got to let me do something." It was always so hard to do something for Aunt Sophie.

"All right, you bring the bread. We'll have stew and bread."

"And Sampson. We'll have Sampson for dinner, too?"

At that she smiled such as I'd never seen from her, even when she'd first began talking about David. Clear, deep in her eyes.

"Yes, Sampson," she agreed. "We'll talk. Then you'll know it all." She rolled her eyes. "Get going now." She whacked the hood of my car with the flat of her broad hand. She made me laugh.

Thinking about her mystery as I made my way through the heavy noon-hour traffic, I was amazed at the number of clues her house held to that past life. The quilt on the upstairs bed with embroidered shells and the outline of Haystack Rock, and two small children at the base looking at the tide pools. The shells in the kitchen. And the booties on the dresser in her bedroom. We'd teased her about a past love, but never seriously. It had been a joke. I wondered now how she had felt when we teased her. "Poor old Aunt Sophie" had always been there for us.

Sure, she supported herself with her sewing machine, doing mending and alterations, and quilting, quilting, quilting, until we wondered that her eyes didn't give out, but no one in the family ever gave it serious consideration. We were proud when she won a first prize at the State Fair one year for a quilt she made out of silk ties, but we never took it as seriously as she did. Even when the demand for her creations took off, so she was able to sell the large backlog that she had and had more work than she had hours for, we counted it as just luck. Never thought of it as art.

What could be more important than our lives, what we thought about this and that? It was Aunt Sophie's purpose to be there for us. We never questioned it. I'd been as selfish as Len was. What made us happy should make her happy too.

After work I headed to her house for dinner and story. My thoughts returned to her when I stopped at the deli for bread. How about a hearty rye? Not what we usually had with her stew, and not something I would have bought for her before, though I was fond of it. Now I thought of her in a different way. A woman with experience in the varieties of life, indeed more experience than I, a twentieth century woman.

When I pulled into her driveway I saw another car there, a blue Land Cruiser with a tracing of rust on the bumpers. It had the look somehow of a traveling vehicle, a practical but fun wagon. Stickers from tourist places--Trees of Mystery, Grand Canyon, et cetera--on the back window.

No one in the family owned a car like that.

I grabbed up my purse, camera and the sack of bread. I heard a whisper of voices from inside and rapped lightly. Aunt Sophie didn't answer.

I figured she couldn't hear me so I turned the knob and walked in. "Hello? Aunt Sophie?"

My heart was pounding and it irritated me. This was my Aunt's house. No strange voices should be here and getting me so nervous.

The front door opened onto her living room where there was a couch and a couple easy chairs. On the couch were a man's jacket, a paper bag, a small suitcase. Hmmm.

I went on through to the dining room. No one there, so I dropped the bread onto the table. The voices came again, a male voice, and Aunt Sophie answering. It sounded like they were outside, beyond the kitchen. I left my purse and camera on the kitchen counter and followed the voices through the kitchen and out the screen door.

Aunt Sophie and a man both knelt by the flower bed just beyond the back door. He was digging with a trowel. Aunt Sophie was holding a jar of water out to him as I approached, noticed by neither of them.

He laid the trowel aside and reached into a short bucket at his left, fishing for a plant I could see but didn't immediately recognize.

From the doorway, I said, "Aunt Sophie, what'cha doing?"

They both jumped, and water sloshed from Aunt Sophie's jar. They turned to look at me, so that their faces were side by side. I saw double.

He was Sophie's son, no doubt about it.

The angular faces were the same, the hair swept back so that the little peak at the hairline showed. Hers was white, his still mostly black but with some gray streaks, and a little longer than the norm for men his age, but full and bushy ending right at the nape of his neck. A long neck, like Aunt Sophie's.

Both pairs of blue eyes looked at me, both mouths smiled.
They were comfortable with each other in the garden, where the
sun shined and the birds chirped.

"Oh, my." It was all I could say.

They both laughed.

"You're just in time, Annie," Aunt Sophie gestured towards
the wooden path that ran through her garden. "Set yourself down
while we finish planting these wild strawberries. Sam brought
them to me from home."

Home? I was unsettled by her reference. Aunt Sophie belongs
to me--this is her home. With an inner shake to straighten myself
out, I sat on the lawn. In moments I felt grounded again. She was
still mine. Then she presented him to me as a bonus, her surprise.

"Annie, meet your cousin, Jonathan Sampson Smithers. My
son."

I know my eyes went wide at "My son", even though it was
obvious.

With scarcely a breath she added, "Sam, this is your cousin
Annie, my favorite niece."

I laughed. "She says that to all of us. 'Course she really means
it with me."

"I'd shake your hand," Sampson said, in a strong but gentle
voice--was I hearing an echo of David? "But you can see, I'm busy.
Mom just couldn't wait to get these in the ground."

I heard the "Mom" and was glad they didn't hear my gasp.

"He brought them up from the cabin," Aunt Sophie said, in a
voice I'd never heard, edged as it was with a maternal and, yes, an
ownership tone. "One of the last patches left, as most of it is grass
now he tells me. A proper lawn." She sighed.

Sampson took the jug from her and poured the water into the hole. He scooped up the rest of the berry plants and arranged them in the muddy row.

"Don't you have a hose around here?" He looked around.

I jumped up to get the hose from where it was curled up at the side of the house. I turned it on to a slow stream and brought it to him. After firming the ground around the berry plants, he added water until it ran off into the grass.

They both leaned back and said, "There," at the same time. We all laughed.

"Annie," Aunt Sophie said, "help me up." I gave her my arm and Sampson steadied her under her other arm.

"Sampson! That's enough water. Let's go wash up, and eat." He got up, more easily than she, but he wasn't young, either. Just how old was he? Born around, what, 1920 wasn't it?

He rejected her outstretched hand, "Thanks, Mom. I got it." And he did. A minute's calculations reminded me that he was over fifty-five, an old guy. It seemed odd that Aunt Sophie's baby could be old.

He was taller than she by about six inches.

From his pants pocket he pulled a handkerchief and wiped his hands. Stained but cleaned of the mud, he reached his right hand out to me. "A proper hello, cousin Annie. I've heard a lot about you."

Aunt Sophie busied herself rolling up the hose to put back at the side of the house, but she was attentive, threw me a little smile.

"And I've heard a lot about you."

"I 'spect you have." He gathered up the trowel and the pad Aunt Sophie had kneeled on. He looked around for where to put them.

I was proud to be able to show him where we put the tools.

"Over here, in the little shed Uncle Boyd built for Aunt Sophie." I opened the door to the shed. "We put them here."

We. Our. I liked using those ownership words. And then felt silly at myself. I kept talking as I put the things on a shelf and came back out. He closed the door with the little peg-latch.

"But most of what I know about you is of you as a baby and little kid."

Aunt Sophie opened the screen door to the house, waving us in before her.

"Yes, Sam." Aunt Sophie started to shut the door and then left it open for air. "Annie doesn't know much about you now, about what happened to you after the war."

"Oh, she doesn't want to hear all of that." He looked at me. "You don't want to hear all that?"

I just shrugged at him, trying to be agreeable with this stranger with whom I felt so familiar.

"Long ago and too much history. Old history."

"Well, something. How about now? You're married? Children? Do you still have the cabin? Can I see it?" I hardly gave him time to answer.

"Whoa," he laughed. "Sweet Sue. Two boys, but they're not little. Yes, and of course."

All the while I was thinking, I need my camera. But I let the camera lay--too intrusive.

"I have pictures I can show you after dinner. Sue and I have some cottages that we built with Dad and Mother Amy, on the property where Mom's cottage was. Dad named them 'Sophie's Cabins.'

"When the war was over, I studied agriculture at Oregon State. Sue was in school there in Business Ed, and working in the Ag office. We met. She was a pretty wench. Sue's a farm girl, from Damascus, up by Portland. Raised on her parent's farm, an orchard of primarily prune and peach trees. My very own peach. We married. Mom and Dad loved her, too.

"After graduation I didn't have a job, so we lived on the farm with Sue's parents. Our Davie was born there. It was a good life, and lots of free fruit. Hard work but we liked it. Then Dad, my dad, had one of his ideas, and we moved back home to help my parents build and then run the cabins. It was going to be for just a while, but it became our life. We lived in town; it's a good place to raise a family. Davie's grown and married, with twin girls. Mom and Dad are gone, so now, Sue and I live in their old place. Modernized it some.

"You can stay with us, or in Sophie's Cabins, when you come down."

We pulled out the chairs and sat down at the table where Aunt Sophie had set our places with soup bowls. I'd put the bread on a platter, in the center. She smiled now when she picked up the plate.

"Annie! Rye bread? How clever. Nice to have something different now and then, don't you think?" She directed the latter part of her remarks to Sampson.

"Yes, indeedy." He smiled at her and then at me. "I wondered when she was ever going to let me meet my other family."

"Jonathan." The formal reproach made us both look at her. "You surely understand, it was different times and then... It never seemed the time to just bring you up. Oh, not you." She was stumbling around her words, trying to smooth out the harshness.

"The situation. And I wanted to protect you too." She put down the knife with which she was buttering her bread, and reached out her hand to put over his, "I couldn't stand to see any condemnation of either you or me, or your father. So I lived with it and built a life here without you. And I wish..."

She pulled her hand away and wrung it with the other one before dropping them into her lap. "I wish it could have been different. That I could have been braver."

She put her hands to busy work, spooning stew into our bowls and handing them to us.

"But I wasn't."

"It's okay, Mom." He took his bowl from her.

She sighed again, this time a lighter sound, happy. She began to eat.

Sampson filled the dinner hour with tales of his life in the years between then and now.

He had first come to visit Sophie after the war, a visit which began the healing for both of them. At first, after the tourist season died down, he and Sue brought the boys up and spent a week playing in the city. After they started school, he would come up by himself or they would just come up for the weekend.

The boys knew her as Grandma Sophie.

They stayed in a hotel downtown. Sophie and Sampson recounted the year his sister Lily and family came from Wyoming. They'd all gone to Jantzen Beach Amusement Park, rode the roller coaster, ate cotton candy. Grandma Sophie went up with Sampson and Lillie's children on the Ferris Wheel, even though it scared her to death. She and Lily had hugged in relief when Sophie and the children were back on solid ground.

As they told me the stories, laughing together, I understood that this telling of the whole story to me, with him, was healing something in her that I'd not known was broken.

After dinner he showed me photos of his family, and he let me take a couple of him and Sophie together. It was still light outside, so I got a couple of great shots of the two of them by her new berry patch.

"Oh," she said as we came back into the dim house. "I almost forgot. Turn on some lights, Annie. Sampson, please, the sack."

He handed her the paper bag I'd noticed on the couch when I came through the house, but hadn't thought about once I'd got outside and seen him.

"Here, Annie. Hold the bottom."

I took hold of the sack while she reached in and pulled out the contents.

The quilt.

Sampson and she stretched it out over the back of the couch, arranging it so I could see The Beach In Winter: Haystack Rock, the Fingers, the tide pools, the ocean, the lighthouse shining through the gray sky. It was faded and ragged in places, the binding coming loose around the bottom.

She fussed with it, tucking the binding into place. "Oh, you'll have to leave it with me, it needs some mending." Her fingers traced the edges of Haystack Rock, smoothed an edge of sky where her stitching had come loose.

The Beach in Winter was more beautiful than any other quilt of hers I'd seen. Maybe because I knew the history. The work wasn't as fine as her later prizewinning ones, but there was a life there, in that putting together of pieces of fabric, that still spoke through the wear of the years.

And of course I wanted it, but it was Sampson's. The way he handled it when he helped Aunt Sophie fold it to put it back in the bag to leave with her to mend showed me that. I did get a photo of her with the quilt when she had mended it. It is tucked into the corner of the mirror by the table where I write.

* * * *

The photos and memories are all that I have left of her now.

Cousin Sampson and Sue are important to me. We are good friends as well as relatives with whom we can be honest and open.

That night, after Sampson left and I was getting ready to leave, Aunt Sophie reached for me and hugged me tighter than she ever had. We never talked about it again. She died peacefully in her sleep some years later. I have the box, with the papers still inside, and some other things to remember her by, though I don't need any thing for that.

I thought a lot about her story, and why she told it to me, after keeping it closed within herself for all those years. Perhaps the most amazing thing of all was that after she opened up her secret with me, she told the whole family, in one fell swoop. She took Sampson to the yearly family reunion on Memorial Day.

It's always held at the cemetery where my grandparents are buried. We put flowers on the graves, and then picnic after at a park nearby. Grandmother Mandy was confused and her open mouth was a sight to see. Some of it came with her age, but it appeared to me she was more surprised that such a thing had happened and that she had never known about it. This tickled Aunt Sophie.

"Well, 'Sampson', is it?" As she handed him a plate, you could see she thought his name was odd. "Get yourself something to eat." She waved at the picnic table, and added, apparently as an afterthought, "Join the family."

She walked away muttering, "I don't know why it was such a big secret, Sophie always had to do things her own way, never trusting us." Her children who were there--my dad and a few of his brothers and sisters--were reserved at first. Maybe they felt the way I did maybe, uncertain about our relationships, and our place now in Aunt Sophie's affections. Had the love all those years been a lie? She sure looked happier with Sampson than with us all, but again, was it the fear of being replaced? That faded quickly as we adjusted our family roles to include a nephew, a cousin who was easy going and had a family of his own.

We started feeling rich and happy to have a family member with cabins at the beach that we can rent for less. He didn't want to charge anything but we're not a bunch of freeloaders. However, we are willing to take a break when we can get it.

I stopped seeing Len soon after my weekend with Aunt Sophie. The pull to submit to him was strong. It would have been so easy. But he laughed at me once too often. During the fight that followed, he said, "I don't want you fooling around with that picture business anymore. I don't want a wife who smells like a chemist."

I wasn't sure after that that I wanted to date again, but of course, I did. Now after several cautious years I've found a man who is secure enough in himself to enjoy my love of photography, who knows it's part of me.

We're going down to the beach this weekend, to the cabins, for cousins Sampson and Sue to get a good look at him. Who knows, as we say in the trade, what might develop?

I think Aunt Sophie would like him.

The End

ABOUT THE AUTHOR

Patsy Brookshire loves stories: reading, telling, writing them. Her first novel in Sophie's Kin & Quilt Suspense Series, THREADS, tangles fiction, family history, and bits of herself. Her second novel, SCANDAL AT THE WILLAMINA QUILT SHOW, explores love in our three phases of life: youth, middle and older years. Humor and passion color all her writings. She observes, "Our response to love in its many variations has a way of flipping our perceptions of ourselves. I continue to marvel and laugh at the wondrously crazy things we do for love." The making of a quilt is richly stitched into many of her tales.

For her writing Ms. Brookshire mines her personal history of growing up in Oregon and travels beyond. Her experiences with love, marriage and divorce; love, marriage and widowhood, include the rich vein of mothering to son Greg, daughter Jennifer and her four now-grown grandchildren. She lives on the Oregon coast beside the Pacific Ocean and a protected wetland that she calls The Peaceable Kingdom. It's a beautiful pond populated with little fish, small birds, great blue herons, the occasional elegant white egret, a variety of wild geese and something that makes loud splashes in the night. The many frogs sing her to sleep. She does, of course, write about it.